AF609481

UTTAR PRADESH

A STATE STUDY GUIDE

KEHAR SINGH YADAV

Published by

Hawk Press
4836/24, Ansari Road, Daryaganj
New Delhi – 110 002
Phones: 91-11-23278618, 91-11-43667199
E-mail: thehawkpress@gmail.com
www.thehawkpress.com

ISBN: 978-93-88318-70-9

Preface

Uttar Pradesh is the most populous state of India. It is situated in the northern part of India and shares boundary with Uttarakhand, Bihar, Madhya Pradesh, Rajasthan, Haryana, Delhi, Himachal Pradesh and an international border with Nepal.Here, we are giving important information on Uttar Pradesh, which is very useful as GK study material for the preparation of competitive examinations like UPSC-prelims, SSC, State Services, NDA, CDS, and Railways etc.

Uttar Pradesh preserved its intellectual excellency even under the British administration. The British combined Agra and Oudh into one province, and called it United Provinces of Agra and Oudh. The name was shortened to the United Provinces in 1935. In January 1950, the United Provinces was renamed as Uttar Pradesh.

Uttar Pradesh is India's most populous state with a population 199,581,477 (2011 census). It is divided into 75 districts with Lucknow as its capital. Wheat, rice, sugar cane, apples, mango, pulses, oil seeds and potatoes are the main crops of Uttar Pradesh. Uttar Pradesh boasts of a growing service sector, which include tourism, healthcare, information technology services, financial services and insurance. Uttar Pradesh attracts a large number of tourists. The famous Taj Mahal of Agra is located in this state. It also hosts the world famous 'Kumbh Mela'. It has many state of the art hotels to cater to the lodging needs of visitors, both national and international.

Uttar Pradesh has the largest population of nearly 167 million. Its is also the fifth largest state in terms of land area.

The western plain is the most urban region. Agriculture is the most important section of the UP's economy, employing about three-fourths of the work force. Uttar Pradesh has the largest production of food grain and oil seeds in India. In addition, UP ranks the first in the production of wheat, maize, barley, gram, sugar cane, and potatoes. The three most important industries of UP are sugar, cotton fabrics and diversified food preparations. Goods carrier equipment, photostat machines, chemicals, polyester fiber and steel tube galvanized sheets are the other big industries of UP.

Uttar Pradesh is an attempt to bring before readers a picturesque presentation of history, geography, divisions and districts, state policies for development and incentives, economy and tourism destinations, inter alia numerous other details. The state encompasses world famous Taj Mahal, Holy Rivers Ganga and Yamuna, many famous mosques, forts, temples, Buddhist religious places, wildlife, rich biodiversity, parks, sanctuaries, vivid cultures, arts, crafts, music and dance styles, abundant natural and mineral resources, etc.

This is a reference book. All the matter is just compiled and edited in nature, taken from the various sources which are in public domain.

This panoramic presentation on various facets of Uttar Pradesh will be of immense help and guide to students, teachers, tourists, guides and general readers.

—Editor

ABOUT THE BOOK

The importance of Uttar Pradesh in India's socio-political firmament is never overstated. That evolves naturally on account of a variety factors, which includes its position as the most populous State in the country and the consequent influence wielded by its people and their leadership in the nation's polity. Uttar Pradesh is a state in northern India. Abbreviated as UP, it is the most populous state in the Republic of India as well as the most populous country subdivision in the world. The densely populated state, located in the northern region of the Indian subcontinent, has over 200 million inhabitants. It was created on 1 April 1937 as the United Provinces of Agra and Oudh during British rule, and was renamed Uttar Pradesh in 1950. On 9 November 2000, a new state, Uttarakhand, was carved out from the state's Himalayan hill region. The two major rivers of the state, the Ganges and Yamuna, join at Allahabad (Prayagraj) and then flow as the Ganges further east. Hindi is the most widely spoken language and is also the official language of the state. The economy of Uttar Pradesh is the fourth-largest state economy in India with 14.89 lakh crore (US$210 billion) in gross domestic product and a per capita GDP of 55,000 (US$770). Agriculture and service industries are the largest parts of the state's economy. This panoramic presentation on various facets of Uttar Pradesh will be of immense help and guide to students, teachers, tourists, guides and general readers.

Contents

1

State at a Glance

Uttar Pradesh is a state in northern India. Abbreviated as UP, it is the most populous state in the Republic of India as well as the most populous country subdivision in the world. The densely populated state, located in the northern region of the Indian subcontinent, has over 200 million inhabitants. It was created on 1 April 1937 as the United Provinces of Agra and Oudh during British rule, and was renamed *Uttar Pradesh* in 1950. The state is divided into 18 divisions and 75 districts with the capital being Lucknow. The main ethnic group is the Hindavi people, forming the demographic plurality. On 9 November 2000, a new state, Uttarakhand, was carved out from the state's Himalayan hill region. The two major rivers of the state, the Ganges and Yamuna, join at Allahabad (Prayagraj) and then flow as the Ganges further east. Hindi is the most widely spoken language and is also the official language of the state.

The state is bordered by Rajasthan to the west, Haryana, Himachal Pradesh and Delhi to the northwest, Uttarakhand and Nepal to the north, Bihar to the east, Madhya Pradesh to the south, and touches the states of Jharkhand and Chhattisgarh to the southeast. It covers 243,290 square kilometres (93,933 sq mi), equal to 7.33% of the total area of India, and is the fourth-largest Indian state by area. The economy of Uttar Pradesh is the fourth-largest state economy in India with 14.89 lakh crore (US$210 billion) in gross domestic product and a per capita GDP of 55,000 (US$770). Agriculture and service industries are the largest parts of the state's economy. The service sector comprises travel and tourism, hotel industry, real estate, insurance and financial consultancies. President's rule has been imposed in Uttar Pradesh ten times since 1968, for different reasons and for a total of 1,700 days.

The natives of the state are generally called Uttar Bhartiya, or more specifically either Awadhi, Bageli, Bhojpuri, Braji, Bundeli, or Rohilkhandi by their region of origin. Hinduism is practised by more than three-fourths of the population, with Islam being the next largest religious group. Uttar Pradesh was home to powerful empires of ancient and medieval India. The state has several historical, natural, and religious tourist destinations, such as Agra, Varanasi and Allahabad.

HISTORY

Prehistory

Modern human hunter-gatherers have been in Uttar Pradesh since between around 85,000 and 72,000 years ago. There have also been prehistorical finds in Uttar Pradesh from the Middle and Upper Paleolithic dated to 21,000–31,000 years old and Mesolithic/Microlithic hunter-gatherer settlement, near Pratapgarh, from around 10550–9550 BC. Villages with domesticated cattle, sheep, and goats and evidence of agriculture began as early as 6000 BC, and gradually developed between c. 4000 and 1500 BC beginning with the Indus Valley Civilisation and Harappa Culture to the Vedic period and extending into the Iron Age.

Ancient and classical period

The kingdom of Kosala, in the Mahajanapada era, was located within the regional boundaries of modern-day Uttar Pradesh. According to Hindu legend, the divine king Rama of the Ramayanaepic reigned in Ayodhya, the capital of Kosala. Krishna, another divine king of Hindu legend, who plays a key role in the Mahabharata epic and is revered as the eighth reincarnation (Avatar) of the Hindu god Vishnu, is said to have been born in the city of Mathura, in Uttar Pradesh. The aftermath of the Mahabharata yuddh is believed to have taken place in the area between the Upper Doab and Delhi, (in what was Kuru Mahajanapada), during the reign of the Pandava king Yudhishthira. The kingdom of the Kurus corresponds to the Black and Red Ware and Painted Gray Ware culture and the beginning of the Iron Age in northwest India, around 1000 BC.

Rama portrayed as an exile in the forest, accompanied by his wife Sita and brother Lakshmana

Control over Gangetic plains region was of vital importance to the power and stability of all of India's major empires, including the Maurya (320–200 BC), Kushan (AD 100–250), Gupta (350–600), and Gurjara-Pratihara (650–1036) empires. Following the Huns' invasions that broke the Gupta empire, the Ganges-Yamuna Doab saw the rise of Kannauj. During the reign of Harshavardhana(590–647), the Kannauj empire reached its zenith. It spanned from Punjab in the north and Gujarat in the west to Bengal in the east and Odisha in the south. It included parts of central India, north of the Narmada River and it encompassed the entire Indo-Gangetic plain. Many communities in various parts of India claim descent from the migrants of Kannauj. Soon after Harshavardhana's death, his empire disintegrated into many kingdoms, which were invaded and ruled by the Gurjara-Pratihara empire, which challenged Bengal's Pala Empire for control of the region. Kannauj was several times invaded by the south Indian Rashtrakuta Dynasty, from the 8th century to the 10th century.

Vedic Period

There is hardly any mention of the area comprising present Uttar Pradesh in Vedic hymns. Even the sacred rivers, the Ganga and Yamuna, appear only on the distance horizon of the land of the Aryans. In the later Vedic age, the importance of Sapta Sindhu recedes and Brahmarshi Desh or Madhya Desh assumes significance. The region comprising Uttar Pradesh at that time became a holy place of India and foremost centre of Vedic culture and knowledge.

The new States of Kuru-Panchal, Kashi and Kosal find mention in late-Vedic texts as prominent centres of Vedic culture. The people of Kuru-Panchat were regarded as the best representatives of Vedic culture. They enjoyed great respect as outstanding orators of Sanskrit. The conduct of schools and institutions by them was laudable. The life of their kinds was a model for other kings and their Brahmins were held in high esteem for their piety and scholarship. The Upanishads prominently mention the Panchal Parishad. The scholars from Kuru-Panchal were specially visited by the Videsh king on the occasion of Ashwamedh Yajna.

The Panchal king Pravahan Jaivali himself was a great thinker who was praised even by Brahmin scholars like Shilik, Dalabhya, Shvetketu and his father Uddalak Aruni. Ajatshatru of Kashi was another great-philosopher king whose superiority was acknowledged by Brahmin scholars like Dripti, Valhaki, Gargya etc., Literature in various disciplines was authored on an extensive scale during this age culminating in the Upanishads. They signify the highest reach of human imagination.

The Upanishad literature was the product of meditation in the Ashrams of the sages, several of which were in Uttar Pradesh, Eminent sages like Bharadwaj, Yajnavalkya, Vashishta, Valmiki and Atri have either their Ashrams here or were otherwise connected with this State. Some Aranyans and Upanishads were, in written in the Ashrams located in this State.

Post-Vedic Period

The cultural heritage of Uttar Pradesh was maintained in the period of the Ramayana and Mahabharat *i.e.* the epic period. The story of Ramayana revolves round the Ikshwaku dynasty of Kosal and of Mahabharat a round the 'Kuru' dynasty of Hastinapur. Local people firmly believe that the Ashram of Valmiki, the author of Ramayana, was in Brahmavart (Bithoor in Kanpur District) and it was in the surroundings of Naimisharany (Nimsar-Misrikh in Sitapur district) that Suta narrated the story of Mahabharat as he had heard it from Vyasji.

Some of the Smritis and Puranas were also written in this State. Gautam Buddha, Mahavir, Makkhaliputta Goshal and great thinkers brought about a revolution in Uttar Pradesh in 6th century B.C. Out of these, Makkhaliputta Goshal, who was born at Shravan near Shravasti, was the founder of Ajivika sect.

Mahavir, the 24th Trithankar of Jains was born in Bihar but had a large number of followers in Uttar Pradesh. He is said to have lived twice during rainy season in this State-once in Shravasti and the second time in Padrauna near Deoria. Pawa proved to be his last resting place. In fact, Jainism had entrenched itself in this State even before the arrival of Mahavir. Several Tirthankars such as Parshwanath, Sambharnath and Chandraprabha were born in different cities in this State and attained 'Kaivalya' here Jainism must have retained its popularity in this State in Subsequent centuries also. This fact is borne by the ruins of several ancient temples buildings, etc. The remains of a magnificent Jain Stupa have been dug out near Kankali Tila in Mathura, while Jain shrines built in early middle Age are still preserved in Deogarh, Chanderi and other places.

The Age of Buddha

The founder of Buddhism, Gautam the Buddha, was born in Lumbini in Nepal. His father, King Shuddodhan, was the ruler of a small State, Kapilvastu (now in Siddharthnagar district). His mother, Maya, belonged to the ruling family of another small state, Deodah (now in Deoria district).

The Buddha attained Enlightenment at Bodh Gaya in Bihar but it was in Isipattan or Mrigdav in Sarnath in U.P. that the preached his first sermon and laid the foundation of his Order. From this point of view, Sarnath has the distinction of being the birth place of 'Dhamma' and 'Sangha', the two elements of the Holy Trinity of Buddism, the third being the Buddha himself. Other notable places in Uttar Pradesh followed by Buddha's association are Kushinara of Kushinagar (in Deoria district) where he attained 'Mahaparinirvana, Shravasti the capital of Kisal where he performed a great miracle, and Sankashyar Sankisa (in Etah district) where another miracle of his life occurred. The rulers of several states in the then Uttar Pradesh were greatly influenced by the teaching of Buddha.

The People of the State also did not lag behind in showing love and devotion to the Tathagat, greater part of whose monastic life was spent in Uttar Pradesh. Thus it will be no exaggeration to describe Uttar Pradesh as the Cradle of Buddhism. Besides Buddhism and Jainism, Pauranic Brahmanism also had deep roots in the state. Ancient images of Gods and Goddesses of Brahmanical order, a temple of Kushan period has been found which alludes to Brahmanism. In fact Mathura can be said to be the birthplace of Indian sculpture. Other temples of this faith built in different periods are in Varanasi, Allahabad, Ballia, Ghazipur. Jhansi and Kanpur.

Middle Age of Synthesis

In successive centuries after Buddha, Ayodhya, Prayag, Varanasi, Mathura and several other cities continued to play important role in the making of religious and cultural history in India. Several kings who ruled the region became immortal because of Vedic rituals performed by them and patronage extended by them to learning.

Scholars like Ashwaghosh, Kalidas, Ban, Mayur, Diwakar, Vakpati, Bhavbhuti, Rajshekhar, Laxmidhar, Sri Harsh and Krishna Misra adorned their courts. Yuan-chwang says that the people of Uttar Pradesh were full masters of the language and spoke it correctly, there pronunciation was like that of the Devas, elegant, beautiful, and their intonation clear and district, worthy of emulation by others, the rules framed be these people were accepted by all. Rajashekhar of Pratihar also payas homage in the similar vein to the people and poets of Panchal.

Varanasi continued to be a prominent centre of learning as in the past. Ayodhya and Mathura acquired femmes birth places of Ram and Krishna. Pilgrims from every corner of the country continued to throng to Prayag and as such it was called the Tirtharaj Similarly, the north mountain region, where Kailash and Mansarovar are situated and from where the holy rivers of the country originate, also remained sacred for the piligrims.

The Shankaracharya established one of the four prominent sacred Dhams in Badrikashram in this region.

Middle Age

The liberal traditions continued to flourish in Uttar Pradesh in the middle age as well. Varanasi remained a prominent centre of Hindu learning and Jaunpur, under the Sharqi rulers, a prominent centre of Islamic culture. Jaunpur was describing as the 'Shiraz' of India.

The Sharqi rulers were patrons of music also and there were many famous musicians in their court. Brij region was an important centre of devotional music in those days. It was in Uttar Pradesh that 'Sufis' took inspiration from Hindu thought and philosophy. Ramanand and his famous disciple Kabir and other saints like Ravidas, Darya Shah and Guru Gorakhnath were some of the great men of those times who gave a new direction to the life and culture of this State.

The Hindu teachers laid emphasis on monotheism (oneness of God) and focused attention on the meaninglessness of the caste system. The Muslim sufis were greatly influenced by mysticism. All these saint-poets contributed to the enrichment of both Hindi and Urdu literature. A notable contribution was made by Sultan Feroz Tughlaq who got Sankrit works translated into Presian among the authors of this age, Zia-ud-din Barni will always be held in high esteem.

The tradition of cultural synthesis, which was started by the sufis and saints during the rule of Sultans received great impetus during the reign of wise Mughals. It was a time when a distinct liberal outlook was discernible in all the spheres of human life such as religion, art and literatures.

Many Madaras and Makatabs were opened for muslim education and Varanasi became the traditional centre of Hindu education. Hindi and Urdu literatures developed further and work of translation of Sanskrit books into persian gained momentum. Tulsidas, Surdas, Keshavdas, Bhushan, Malik Muhammad Jayasi, Raskhan, Matiram, Ghananand, Bihari, Dev and Giridhar Kavirai were some of the great poets who brought into being, laurels to Uttar Pradesh. After the disintegration of the Mughal empire, smaller states which came also pursued a policy of giving patronage to poets and musicians.

Architecture, Art and Craft

Several styles of architecture can be seen in Uttar Pradesh. There are buildings built in the Hindu Buddhist styles and Royal memorials and monuments of Indo-Islamic architecture Buildings constructed in Avadh and Sharqi styles of architecture are also remarkable.

In the Jatakas and other ancient works, we find description of several such cities, palaces and forts, which were at sometime situated within the confines of Uttar Pradesh and of which there is not trace now. Almost the similar fate met the Stupas, etc., which were built by Shakya, Malla and other rulers in this State in 6th century B.C. The famous Jain stupa whose ruins have been found in Kankali Tila in Mathura was also built during this period.

Uttar Pradesh in one of the most ancient cradles of Indian culture. While it is true that no Harappa and Mohan-Jodaro have been discovered in the State, the antiquities found in Banda (Bundelkhand), Mirzapur and Meerut link its History to early Stone Age and Harappan era. Chalk drawings or dark red Drawings by primitive men are extensively found in the Vindhyan ranges of Mirzapur districts. Utensils of that age have also been discovered in Atranji-Khera, Kaushambi, Rajghat and Sonkh. Copper articles have been found in Kanpur, Unnao, Mirzapur, Mathura and advent of the Aryans in this State. It is most probable that snapped links between the Indus Valley and Vedic civilizations lie buried under the ruins of ancient sites found in this State.

The Mauryan Period

With the emergence of the Mauryans in 3rd century B.C., a new chapter was opened in the history of Art. It is said that Ashok visited Sarnath and Kushinagar and had personally ordered for construction of Stupas and Viharas at these two sacred places. Their traces have disappeared but the remnants of stone pillars found at Sarnath, Allahabad, Merut, Kausambi, Sankisa and Varanasi give us an idea of the excellence of Mauryan Art. All the Ashokan pillars have been built with Chunar stones.

The Lion Capital of Sarnath is without doubt and excellent specimen of Mauryan Art. Writes the famous historian Vincent Smith, 'It would be difficult to find in any country an example of ancient animal sculpture, superior or even equal to this artistic expression of Sarnath, because it successfully combines realistic treatment with idealistic dignity and every detail has Come out with utmost perfection.' Mathura was another important centre of Art in the Mauryan Period. Colossal sculptures of Yakshas and Yakshinis have been found in the district Parkham, Borada and Jhing-ks-nagar and certain other places.

All these represent contemporary folk art. There was considerable artistic activity in Uttar Pradesh during Shung-Satvahan Period. A large number of architectural and other fragments found in the ruins of Sarnath tell us the story of buildings, etc. built during this period. The remains of a semi-circular temple of this period is now represented only by its foundation wall, During those days Mathura was a prominent centre of Bharhut-Sanchi School of Art. Several important specimens of this schools have been found here.

The Art of Mathura

The Mathura Schools of Art reached its pinnacle during the Kushan Period. The Most important work of this period is the anthromorphic image of the Buddha who was hitherto represented by certain symbols. The artists of Mathura and Gandha were pioneers who carved out images of the Buddha. Images of Jain Tirthankars and Hindu deities were also made in Mathura. Generally, all these initial images were huge in size. Their excellent specimens are still preserved in the museums at Lucknow, Varanasi, Allahabad and Mathura. Colossal images, in seated or standing postures, of Kushan emperors Vim Kadphises and Kanishk and Saka ruler Chashtan have also been found at Math in Mathura district.

They are stated to have been installed in dev-kul (probably a place for worship of ancestors). There is not doubt that Mathura was the centre of manufacturing of stone images (sculpture) during the Kushan Period. These images had a great demand in other parts of the country. Scenes depicted on Stone pillars found in Bhuteshwar and other places in Mathura district present glimpses of contemporary life including dresses, ornaments, means of entertainment, arms, household furniture, etc.

Stone carvings of intoxicated groups of people that have been found, speak about foreign (Hellenistic) influence on this school of art. Considerable construction activities have come to notice in Sarnath also in Kushan Period, ruins of several monasteries, temples and Stupas of that period lie catered there even today.

Delhi Sultanate

Parts or all of Uttar Pradesh were ruled by the Delhi Sultanate for 320 years (1206–1526). Five dynasties ruled over the Delhi Sultanate sequentially: the Mamluk dynasty (1206–90), the Khalji dynasty (1290–1320), the Tughlaq dynasty (1320–1414), the Sayyid dynasty (1414–51), and the Lodi dynasty (1451–1526).

Medieval and early modern period

In the 16th century, Babur, a Timurid descendant of Timur and Genghis Khan from Fergana Valley (modern-day Uzbekistan), swept across the Khyber Pass and founded the Mughal Empire, covering India, along with modern-day Afghanistan, Pakistan and Bangladesh. The Mughals were descended from Persianised Central Asian Turks (with significant Mongol admixture). In the Mughal era, Uttar Pradesh became the heartland of the empire. Mughal emperors Babur and Humayun ruled from Delhi. In 1540 an Afghan, Sher Shah Suri, took over the reins of Uttar Pradesh after defeating the Mughal king Humanyun. Sher Shah and his son Islam Shah ruled Uttar Pradesh from their capital at Gwalior. After the death of Islam Shah Suri, his prime minister Hemu became the *de facto* ruler of Uttar Pradesh, Bihar, Madhya Pradesh, and the western parts of Bengal. He was bestowed the title of *Hemchandra Vikramaditya* (title of Vikramâditya adopted from Vedic Period) at his formal coronation took place at Purana Quila in Delhi on 7 October 1556.A month later, Hemu died in the Second Battle of Panipat, and Uttar Pradesh came under Emperor Akbar's rule. Akbar ruled from Agra and Fatehpur Sikri. In the 18th century, after the fall of Mughal authority, the power vacuum was filled by the Maratha Empire, in the mid-18th century, the Maratha army invaded the Uttar Pradesh region, which resulted in Rohillas losing control of Rohilkhand to the Maratha forces led by Raghunath Rao and Malharao Holkar. The conflict between Rohillas and Marathas came to an end on 18 December 1788 with the arrest of Ghulam Qadir, the grandson of Najeeb-ud-Daula, who was defeated by the Maratha general Mahadaji Scindia. In 1803, following the Second Anglo-Maratha War, when the British East India Company defeated the Maratha Empire, much of the region came under British suzerainty.

British India era

Starting from Bengal in the second half of the 18th century, a series of battles for north Indian lands finally gave the British East India Company accession over the state's territories. Ajmer and Jaipur kingdoms were also included in this northern territory, which was named the "North-Western Provinces" (of Agra). Although UP later became the fifth-largest state of India, NWPA was one of the smallest states of the British Indian empire. Its capital shifted twice between Agra and Allahabad.

Due to dissatisfaction with British rule, a serious rebellion erupted in various parts of North India, which became known as the Indian Rebellion of 1857; Bengal regiment's sepoy stationed at Meerut cantonment, Mangal Pandey, is widely considered as its starting point. After the revolt failed, the British divided the most rebellious regions by reorganising their administrative boundaries, splitting the Delhi region from 'NWFP of Agra' and merging it with Punjab, while the Ajmer-Marwar region was merged with Rajputana and Oudh was incorporated into the state. The new state was called the North Western Provinces of Agra and Oudh, which in 1902 was renamed as the United Provinces of Agra and Oudh. It was commonly referred to as the United Provinces or its acronym UP.

In 1920, the capital of the province was shifted from Allahabad to Lucknow. The high court continued to be at Allahabad, but a bench was established at Lucknow. Allahabad continues to be an important administrative base of today's Uttar Pradesh and has several administrative headquarters. Uttar Pradesh continued to be central to Indian politics and was especially important in modern Indian history as a hotbed of the Indian independence movement. Uttar Pradesh hosted modern educational institutions such as the Benaras Hindu University, Aligarh Muslim University and the Darul Uloom Deoband. Nationally known figures such as Ram Prasad Bismil and Chandra Shekhar Azad were among the leaders of the movement in Uttar Pradesh, and Motilal Nehru, Jawaharlal Nehru, Madan Mohan Malaviya and Gobind Ballabh Pant were important national leaders of the Indian National Congress. The All India Kisan Sabha(AIKS) was formed at the Lucknow session of the Congress on 11 April 1936, with the famous nationalist Swami Sahajanand Saraswatielected as its first President, in order to address the longstanding grievances of the peasantry and mobilise them against the zamindari landlords attacks on their occupancy rights, thus sparking the Farmers movements in India. During the Quit India Movement of 1942, Ballia district overthrew the colonial authority and installed an independent administration under Chittu Pandey. Ballia became known as "Baghi Ballia" (Rebel Ballia) for this significant role in India's independence movement.

Post-independence

After India's independence, the United Provinces were renamed "Uttar Pradesh" ("northern province"), preserving UP as the acronym, notification regarding this was done in union gazette on 24 January 1950. The state has provided nine of India's prime ministers, including current Prime Minister Narendra Modi who is MP from Varanasi, which is more than any other state and is the source of the largest number of seats in the Lok Sabha. Despite its political influence since ancient times, its poor record in economic development and administration, poor governance, organised crime and corruption have kept it amongst India's backward states. The state has been affected by repeated episodes of caste and communal violence. In Ayodhya in December 1992 the disputed Babri Mosque was demolished by radical Hindu activists, leading to widespread violence across India. In 2000, northern districts of the state were separated to form the state of Uttarakhand.

CRIME

According to the National Crime Records Bureau (2011 data), Uttar Pradesh has the highest number of crimes among any state in India, but due to its high population, the actual per capita crime rate is low. Because of this, the NCRB states that UP is the third safest state in the country to live in. The value of human development index in Uttar Pradesh has steadily increased over time. The Uttar Pradesh Police, governed by the Department of Home, is the largest police force in the world.

Uttar Pradesh also reported the highest number of deaths—23,219—due to road and rail accidents in 2015, according to NCRB data. This included 8,109 deaths due to careless driving.

Between 2006 and 2010, the state has been hit with three terrorist attacks, including explosions in a landmark holy place, a court and a temple. The 2006 Varanasi bombings were a series of bombings that occurred across the Hindu holy city of Varanasi on 7 March 2006. At least 28 people were killed and as many as 101 others were injured.

In the afternoon of 23 November 2007, within a span of 25 minutes, six consecutive serial blasts occurred in the Lucknow, Varanasi, and Faizabad courts, in which 28 people were killed and several others injured. The blasts came a week after the Uttar Pradesh police and central security agencies busted Jaish-e-Mohammed terrorists who had planned to abduct Rahul Gandhi. The Indian Mujahideen has claimed responsibility for these blasts in an email sent to TV stations five minutes before the blast. Another blast occurred on 7 December 2010, the blast occurred at Sheetla Ghat in Varanasi in which more than 38 people were killed and several others injured.

HEALTHCARE

District Hospital, Kanpur Dehat

Uttar Pradesh has a large public as well as private healthcare infrastructure, but the performance of the state on various health parameters is not encouraging. Although an extensive infrastructural network of Medical and Health services in the government as well as private sectors has been created over the years, the available health infrastructure is inadequate to meet the demand for health services in the state. In 15 years to 2012–13, the population of Uttar Pradesh increased by more than 25 per cent. However, the public health centres, which are the frontline of the government's health care system, decreased by 8 per cent. Smaller sub-centres, the first point of public contact, increased by no more than 2 per cent over the 25 years to 2015, a period when the population grew by more than 51 per cent.

A newborn in Uttar Pradesh is expected to live four years fewer than in the neighboring state of Bihar, five years fewer than in Haryana and seven years fewer than in Himachal Pradesh. Uttar Pradesh contributed to the largest share of almost all communicable and noncommunicable disease deaths, including 48 per cent of all typhoid deaths (2014); 17 per cent of cancer deaths and 18 per cent of tuberculosis deaths (2015). After Assam, Uttar Pradesh has India's second-highest maternal mortality rate, 285 maternal deaths for every 100,000 live births (2013), with 62 percent of pregnant women unable to access minimum ante-natal care.

Around 42 per cent of pregnant women, more than 1.5 million, deliver babies at home. About two-thirds (61 per cent) of childbirths at home in Uttar Pradesh are unsafe. State has the highest child mortality indicators, from the neonatal mortality rate (NNMR) to the under-five mortality rate of 64 children who die per 1,000 live births before five years of age, 35 die within a month of birth, and 50 do not complete a year of life. A third of the rural population in the state has been deprived of primary healthcare infrastructure, according to the norms of the Indian Public Health Standards.

SPORTS

Traditional sports, now played mostly as a pastime, include wrestling, swimming, kabaddi, and track-sports or water-sports played according to local traditional rules and without modern equipment. Some sports are designed to display martial skills such as using a sword or 'Pata' (stick). Due to lack of organised patronage and requisite facilities, these sports survive mostly as individuals' hobbies or local competitive events. Among modern sports, field hockey is popular and Uttar Pradesh has produced some of the finest players in India, including Dhyan Chand and, more recently, Nitin Kumar and Lalit Kumar Upadhyay.

Recently, cricket has become more popular than field hockey. Uttar Pradesh won its first Ranji Trophy tournament in February 2006, beating Bengalin the final. It can also boast of routinely having 3 or 4 players on the national side. Green Park Stadium in Kanpur, the only internationally recognised cricket stadium in the state, has witnessed some of India's most famous victories. Uttar Pradesh Cricket Association (UPCA) has headquarters in Kanpur. An International Cricket Stadium with a capacity of 50,000 spectators, is being set up in the capital city of Uttar Pradesh.

Greater Noida Cricket Stadium is another newly built international cricket stadium. The Buddh International Circuit hosted India's inaugural F1 Grand Prix race on 30 October 2011. The 5.14-kilometre-long (3.19 mile) circuit was designed by German architect and racetrack designer Herman Tilke to compete with other world-class race circuits. However, races were only held three times before being cancelled due to falling attendance and lack of government support. The government of Uttar Pradesh considered Formula One to be entertainment and not a sport, and thus imposed taxes on the event and participants.

2

Culture and Society

CULTURE OF UTTAR PRADESH

The Culture of Uttar Pradesh is an Indian Culture which has its roots in the Hindi and Urdu literature, music, fine arts, drama and cinema. Lucknow, the capital of Uttar Pradesh, has several beautiful historical monuments such as Bara Imambara and Chhota Imambara. It has also preserved the damaged complex of the Oudh-period British Resident's quarters, which are being restored.

Uttar Pradesh attracts large number of visitors, both national and international; with more than 71 million domestic tourists (in 2003) and almost 25% of the All-India foreign tourists visiting Uttar Pradesh, it is one of the top tourist destinations in India. There are two regions in the state where a majority of the tourists go, viz. the *Agra circuit* and the *Hindu pilgrimage circuit.*

The city of Agra, gives access to three World Heritage Sites: Taj Mahal, Agra Fort and the nearby Fatehpur Sikri. Taj Mahal is a mausoleum built by Mughal Emperor Shah Jahan in memory of his beloved wife, Mumtaz Mahal. It is cited as *"the jewel of Muslim art in India and one of the universally admired masterpieces of the world's heritage". Agra Fort is about 2.5 km northwest of its much more famous sister monument, the Taj Mahal. The fort can be more accurately described as a walled palatial city. Fatehpur Sikri was the world-famous 16th century capital city near Agra, built by the Mughal emperor Akbar the Great, whose mausoleum in Agra is also worth a visit.* Dayal Bagh in Agra is a modern-day temple and popular tourist sight. Its lifelike sculptures in marble are unique in India. Agra's dubious modern attractions include Asia's largest Spa as well as Asia's second 6D theatre.

The pilgrimage circuit includes the holiest of the Hindu holy cities on the banks of sacred rivers Ganges and the Yamuna: Varanasi (also considered world's oldest city), Ayodhya(birthplace of Lord Rama), Mathura (birthplace of Lord Krishna), Vrindavan (the village where Lord Krishna spent his childhood), and Allahabad(Prayagraj) (the confluence or 'holy-sangam' of the sacred Ganges-Yamuna rivers).

Culture from cities

Varanasi is widely considered to be one of the oldest cities in the world. It is famous for its ghats (bathing steps along the river), full of pilgrims year round who come to bathe in the sacred Ganges River. Mathura is world-famous for its colourful celebrations of the Holi festival, which attracts many tourists also – thanks partly to the hype, which the Indian film industry has given to this highly entertaining socio-religious festival.

Thousands gather at Allahabad(Prayagraj) to take part in the Magh Mela festival, which is held on the banks of the Ganges. This festival is organised on a larger scale every 12th year and is called the Kumbha Mela, where over 10 million Hindu pilgrims congregate – proclaimed as one of the largest gathering of human beings in the world. Budaun is also a city which attracts thousands of tourists annually. Its religious city with many historical monuments and tombs of many famous people.

The historically important towns of Sarnath and Kushinagar are located not far from Varanasi. Gautama Buddha gave his first sermon at Sarnath after his enlightenment and died at Kushinagar; both are important pilgrimage sites for Buddhists.

Also at Sarnath are the Pillars of Ashoka and the Lion Capital of Ashoka, both important archaeological artefacts with national significance. At a distance of 80 km from Varanasi, Ghazipur is famous not only for its Ganges Ghats but also for the Tomb of British potentate Lord Cornwallis, maintained by the Archaeological Survey of India.

Dance and music

The state is home to a very old tradition in dance and music. During the eras of Guptas and Harsh Vardhan, Uttar Pradesh was a major centre for musical innovation. Swami Haridas was a great saint-musician who championed Hindustani Classical Music. Tansen, the great musician in Mughal Emperor Akbar's court, was a disciple of Swami Haridas.

Kathak, a classical dance form, involving gracefully coordinated movements of feet along with entire body, grew and flourished in Uttar Pradesh. Wajid Ali Shah, the last Nawab of Awadh, was a great patron and a passionate champion of Kathak. Today, the state is home to two prominent schools of this dance form, namely, Lucknow Gharana Moradabad and Banaras Gharana.

Well-known music personalities such as Naushad Ali, Talat Mehmood, Begum Akhtar, Anup Jalota, Baba Sehgal, Shubha Mudgal, Bismillah Khan, Ravi Shankar, Kishan Maharaj,Vikash Maharaj, Hari Prasad Chaurasia, Gopal Shankar Misra, Siddheshwari Devi, Girija Devi and Sir Cliff Richard were originally from Uttar Pradesh.

The region's folk heritage includes songs called rasiya (known and especially popular in Braj), which celebrate the divine love of Radha and Krishna. These songs are accompanied by large drums known as bumb and are performed at many festivals. Other folk dances or folk theater forms include Raslila, Swang, Ramlila (a dramatic enactment of the entire Ramayana), Nautanki, Naqal (mimicry) and Qawwali.

The Bhatkhande Music Institute is situated in Lucknow.

Languages

The common state-languages of Uttar Pradesh are standard Hindi. While standard Hindi (Khari boli) is the official language, several important regional Hindi 'dialects' are spoken in the state and among these are: Awadhi, Bhojpuri, Braj, Bagheli and Bundeli, besides several local dialects that do not have a formal name. Urdu is prominent in Uttar Pradesh as Lucknow was once the centre of Indo-Persianate culture in north India. The language of Lucknow ("Lakhnavi Urdu") is a form of high literary Urdu.

Dr. Parichay Das is path-breaker poet, essayist, creative critic and singer-actor in Bhojpuri-Hindi-Maithili. He was born in Mau nath Bhanjan district 's Rampur Devlaas village. He was Secretary, Hindi Academy, Delhi and Secretary, Maithili-Bhojpuri Academy, Delhi Govt. He has written and edited more than 30 books.

Protected areas

Some of the main natural protected areas in Uttar Pradesh are:-

- Dudhwa National Park is one of the best tiger reserves in the country.
- Pilibhit Tiger Reserve – home to the Tiger Reserve.
- Sandi Bird Sanctuary – houses about 20,000 migratory birds annually.
- Katarniaghat Wildlife Sanctuary – the most concentrated sanctuary in India with a large population of tigers as well as leopards – situated in Bahraich and bordering Nepal is also worth a visit.

Some areas require a special permit for non-Indians to visit.

Dress

The people of Uttar Pradesh wear a variety of native- and Western-style dress. Traditional styles of dress include colourful draped garments – such as sari for women and dhoti or lungi for men – and tailored clothes such as salwar kameez for women and kurta-pyjama for men. Men also often sport a head-gear like topi or pagri. Sherwani is a more formal male dress and is frequently worn along with chooridar on festive occasions. European-style trousers and shirts are also common among the men.

MUSIC AND DANCE

Uttar Pradesh has produced musicians, including Anup Jalota, Girija Devi, Kishan Maharaj Naushad Ali, Ravi Shankar, Shubha Mudgal, Siddheshwari Devi, Talat Mehmood, and Ustad Bismillah Khan. The Ghazal singer Begum Akhtar was a native of Uttar Pradesh. The region's folk heritage includes songs called rasiya (especially popular in Braj), which celebrate the divine love of Radha and Krishna. Other forms of music are kajari, sohar, qawwali, rasiya, thumri, birha, chaiti, and sawani. Traditional dance and musical styles are taught at the Bhatkhande Music Institute University in Lucknow, named after the musician Pandit Vishnu Narayan Bhatkhande.

Kathak, a classical dance form, owes its origin to the state of Uttar Pradesh. The dance form is connected to classical Hindustani music where the rhythmic nimbleness of the feet is accompanied by either Tabla or Pakhawaj. Four of the six schools of this dance form, Lucknow gharana, Ajrara gharana, Farukhabad gharana and Benares gharana, are situated in Uttar Pradesh.

Fairs and festivals

Diwali (celebrated between mid-October and mid-December) and Rama Navami are popular festivals in Uttar Pradesh. Kumbh Mela, organised in the month of Maagha (February—March), is a major festival held every twelve years in rotation at Allahabad, Haridwar, Ujjain, on the river Ganges and Nasik on the Godavari river. Lath mar Holi is a local celebration of the Hindu festival of Holi. It takes place well before the actual Holi in the town of Barsana near Mathura. Taj Mahotsav, held annually at Agra, is a colourful display of the culture of the Braj area.

Hindu priest saluting the sun in the Ganges, Varanasi

Buddha Purnima, which marks the birth of Gautama Buddha, is a major Hindu and Buddhist festival, while Christmas is celebrated by the minority Christian population. Other festivals are Eid-ul-Fitr, Eid-ul-Adhaa/Bakreed, Vijayadashami, Makar Sankranti, Vasant Panchami, Ayudha Puja, Ganga Mahotsava, Janmashtami, Sardhana Christian Fair, Maha Shivaratri, Mahavir Jayanti, Bârah Wafâm□""ÐD", Chhath puja, Lucknow Mahotsav, Moharram, Kabob and Hanuman Jayanti.

CUISINE

Uttar Pradeshi thali with naan, sultani dal, raita, and shahi paneer

Paan, (betel leaves) being served with silver foil

A typical day-to-day traditional vegetarian meal of Uttar Pradesh, like any other North Indian thali, consists of roti (flatbread), chawal, dal, sabji, raita and papad. Many people still drink the traditional drink chaach (traditional Butter milk) with meals. On festive occasions, usually 'tava' (flat pan for roti) is considered inauspicious, and instead fried foods are consumed. A typical festive thali consists of Puri, Kachauri, sabji, pulav, papad, raita, salad and desserts (such as sewai or Kheer).

Many communities have their own particular style of cuisines, such as the Jains, Kayasths and Muslims. There are also certain sub-regional delicacies. Awadhi cuisine is world-famous for dishes such as kebab, biryani, keema and nihari. Sweets occupy an important place in the Hindu diet and are eaten at social ceremonies. People make distinctive sweetmeats from milk products, including khurchan, peda, gulabjamun, petha, makkhan malai, and chamcham. The chaat in Lucknow and Banarasi Paan is known across India for its flavour and ingredients.

Awadhi cuisine is from the city of Lucknow. The cuisine consists of both vegetarian and non-vegetarian dishes. Awadh has been greatly influenced by Mughal cooking techniques, and the cuisine of Lucknow bears similarities to those of Central Asia, Kashmir, Punjab and Hyderabad; and the city is known for Nawabi foods. The bawarchis and rakabdars of Awadh gave birth to the dum style of cooking or the art of cooking over a slow fire, which has become synonymous with Lucknow today. Their spread consisted of elaborate dishes like kebabs, kormas, biryani, kaliya, nahari-kulchas, zarda, sheermal, roomali rotis, and warqi parathas. The richness of Awadh cuisine lies not only in the variety of cuisine but also in the ingredients used like mutton, paneer, and rich spices including cardamom and saffron.

Mughlai cuisine is a style of cooking developed in the Indian subcontinent by the imperial kitchens of the Mughal Empire. It represents the cooking styles used in North India, especially Uttar Pradesh. The cuisine is strongly influenced by the cuisine of Central Asia, and has in turn strongly similarities to the regional cuisines of Kashmir and the Punjab region. The tastes of Mughlai cuisine vary from extremely mild to spicy, and is often associated with a distinctive aroma and the taste of ground and whole spices.

Dress

The people of Uttar Pradesh dress in a variety of traditional and Western styles. Traditional styles of dress include colourful draped garments—such as sari for women and dhotior lungi for men—and tailored clothes such as salwar kameez for women and kurta-pyjama for men. Men often sport head-gear like topi or pagri. Sherwani is a more formal male dress and is frequently worn along with chooridar on festive occasions. European-style trousers and shirts are also common among the men.

Media

A number of newspapers and periodicals are published in Hindi, English, and Urdu. *The Pioneer* was founded in Allahabad in 1865 by George Allen. *Amar Ujala*, *Dainik Bhaskar*, *Dainik Jagran*, *Rajasthan Patrika* and *Hindustan Dainik* have a wide circulation, with local editions published from several important cities. Major English language newspapers which are published and sold in large numbers are *The Telegraph*, *The Times of India*, *Hindustan Times*, *The Hindu*, *The Statesman*, *The Indian Express*, and *Asian Age*. Some prominent financial dailies like

The Economic Times, *Financial Express*, *Business Line*, and *Business Standard* are widely circulated. Vernacular newspapers such as those in Hindi, Nepali, Gujarati, Odia, Urdu, and Punjabi are also read by a select readership.

Doordarshan is the state-owned television broadcaster. Multi system operators provide a mix of Hindi, English, Bengali, Nepali and international channels via cable. Hindi 24-hour television news channels are *NDTV India*, *DD News*, *Zee News Uttar Pradesh*, *Jan TV*, *IBN-7*, and *ABP News*. *All India Radio* is a public radio station. There are 32 private FMstations available in major cities like Lucknow, Kanpur, Varanasi, Allahabad, Agra, and Noida. Cell phone providers include *Vodafone*, *Airtel*, *BSNL*, Reliance Jio, *Reliance Communications*, *Telenor*, *Aircel*, *Tata Indicom*, *Idea Cellular*, and *Tata DoCoMo*. Broadband internet is available in select towns and cities and is provided by the state-run BSNL and by private companies. Dial-up access is provided throughout the state by BSNL and other providers.

VILLAGE SCENES

The village is the lynch-pin of the state's economy. An assorted, shapeless cluster of mud huts, roofed with thatch or khaprail (earthen tiles) with hardly any sanitation, drainage or lighting arrangements and only narrow footpaths leading to the outside world constitute a typical Uttar Pradesh village.

Times has had little effect on the shape or architecture of the Uttar Pradesh village. Near cities, signs of prosperity increase. Houses belonging to the prosperous farmers was plastered with cement and reinforced brick-work roofs or arched doors and windows.

Land is the status symbol in the village while the landowners generally are from the higher castes, it is their position as land owners which gives them status and power rather than their caste affiliation. Dire poverty and pressure on land impelled the lower caste people of eastern districts of Uttar Pradesh towards the end of the nineteenth century to migrate to distant lands and forced people into deviations from the traditional norms.

Since Independence, the concept of welfare state, Zamindari abolition, the latest result of science and technology has benefited the village. Some well-placed educated city-dwellers have taken to the land. All this has changed the traditional concept of village as a self-sufficient unit where the requisite complement of occupational caste workers was always available to meet the needs of the villagers from birth to death. In a survey in the mid-Gangetic valley it was found that no single caste occurred in all the villages surveyed. Chamars, Ahirs, Brahmins, Nai, Lohars, Telis, Dhobis, Kurmis, Kumhars and Baniyas were found in the villages.

The Nai (barber) is a journeyman who goes from door to door and village to village and can minister to the wants of more than one village. Dhobis are scarce because they cater primarily to the upper castes. Baniyas are as sparely scattered as the Dhobis because a single Baniya can finance operations within a radius of 10 to 20 miles or more.

It is not only the lower castes that have abandoned their jajmani (Its a system where services are returned in goods or reciprocal services) obligations. The Brahmins have also done so. They formerly used to officiate at marriages and other ceremonies at the homes of their jajmans and received the traditional offerings in money and goods. The village Brahmins have given up some of their traditional functions. They regard as demeaning the practice of accepting food and charity or settling marriages, cooking food at wedding and officiating as priests. Some of the Brahmins have taken to cultivation and other occupations, such as tailoring and shop-keeping. The exploitative situations exists in other areas where the jajmani system still prevails.

A marriage in the village is a high point in its social life. There is much ostentatious display and expenditure of money by the family concerned. All the occupational castes, gets involved with the wedding through well defined customs, rules and regulations. It provides an occasion for the caste-men to strengthen their ties with the jajman.

To a lesser degree the same is the case with funeral and the other major samskaras an upper caste Hindu goes through in his life-cycle. These are mundan when the child's head is shaved off, janaeoo or investiture of sacred thread and vidyarambha or initiation into student life. The expenditure involved in rites and rituals from birth to death keeps most of the families perpetually in debt.

An occasional dangel (wrestling bout) or inter-village kabaddi match can keep the village agog for a long time. A form of the folk theatre (nautanki), the village puppet show (kathputli) and the recitation in the rainy season of the heroic deeds of two Bundela warriors (Alah-Udal) are longed for events. Bazars are held weekly, bi-weekly or tri-weekly at suitable points from where the villages obtain their house hold requirements. A three-tier democracy is at work in the countryside. At the district level is the Zila Parishad, at the block level the Kshetra Samiti and at the village level, the Panchayat. To solve minor disputes there is the Nyaya Panchayat or the village court. All these are statutory bodies and form what is called the Panchayati Raj. Election to the Panchayats is by adult franchise and secret direct vote. Election to the Kshetra Samities is by indirect vote, Panchayat in a block constituting the electoral college.

The Zila Parishad has both ex-officio members and elected members. The ex-officio members include the members of Parliament, Assembly and the council of the district. A lot of Government money in the shape of loans, assistance and advances for rural development is funneled through these institutional bodies into the villages.

The emergence of political bosses at the grass-root level is a new development in village life. Together with prosperous farmers and caste leaders they constitute the new rural elite. The Nyaya Panchayat perform certain statutory functions in village disputes but it is the caste Panchayats among the backward classes and the scheduled castes which are more formidable. Most caste disputes are settled by them. These caste Panchayat also perform certain other functions. They help to alleviate the difficulties of poor families to some extent, fixing limits to dowries, the number of persons to participate in marriage party and so on. They also regulate the customary dues involved in the system of Jajmani relationship.

CULTURAL HERITAGE

Hindu civilization and culture reached its apogee in the territory of Uttar Pradesh. Some scholars are of the view that the Rig Veda was composed in the Gangetic valley. But even if this be not true, it is generally accepted that a substantial portion of the Vedic literature had its origin here in its many hermitages, which were seats of learning. Some of the big names in Hindu sacred literature, such as Yajnavalkya, Vashishtha, Vishvamitra, Valmiki, Attriyea, Bharadwaja, Kapil and Vyas lived in these sylvan retreats of Uttar Pradesh and inspired millions through the ages.

Uttar Pradesh's greatest gifts to humanity are the two epics, 'Ramayana' and 'Mahabharata'. From the epic age, the territory of Uttar Pradesh being watered by several fresh streams of culture, the two most significant being those generated by the teachings of the Buddha and Mahavira, the 24th Jain Tirthankar. Manifestations of these are to be found in a mass of literature and numerous relics of art and architecture which form part of the precious cultural heritage of the country. Brahmanical culture eclipsed by the more virile and vigorous Buddhism.

Culture in all its manifestations served the ends of religion. The fountainheads of Brahmanical culture were centrad at holy places as Kashi, Ayodhya, Prayag, Mathura and the Himalayan hermitages. Mathura has proved to be a veritable store-house of buried ancient art, both of the Brahmanical and Buddhist varieties and Kashi, which has withstood the ravages of times, of living Hindu art.

There was an efflorescence of Buddhist art during the reign of Ashoka and of Hindu art during the Golden Age of the Guptas. The invasion by the Greeks a little earlier and during this period supplied the necessary leaven for art and literature to flourish. Secular literature was not neglected and included poetry, drama, lyric, prose, romance and fables.

There are several writers whose work have earned distinction and renown. Some of them are Asvaghosha of Ayodhya of Buddha Charita fame, Harishena, the author of the Allahabad Prasasti, Vakapatiraja of Kannauj and Bhavabhuti in Vashovarman's court and Bana Bhatta, the court-poet of Emperor Harsha and author of Kadambari. By the beginning of the seventh century AD, Hinduism had revived sufficiently to cripple Buddhism.

Hindu temples outnumbered Buddhist monasteries in an increasing proportion. Shankaracharya further weakened this dying institutions, but the death-blow was dealt by the early Muslim who razed their monasteries - the last ditch positions which the Buddhist held against resurgent Hinduism.

Buddhism ceased to be an effective instrument of culture in the country after this. Then began the dark Middle Ages for Hindu culture. Vandalism was let loose on the land by the fanatical Muslim rulers. Art and culture came to a grinding halt. Some compulsory contacts had to be maintained between the attacker and the attacked through a spoken word. The result was the development of Hindu and the birth of Urdu as Hindustani or rekhta. Music found its votaries among Muslims. Muslim building activity led to a synthesis of architecture which is styled as Indo-Saracen. New industries, arts and crafts, came up including shawl-making, inlay work, brocade, muslin, carpet-weaving, paper-making etc.

SOCIETY AND CULTURE

Uttar Pradesh in one of the most ancient cradles of Indian culture, while it is true that no Harappa and Mohan-Jodaro have been discovered in the State, the antiquities found in Banda (Bundelkhand), Mirzapur and Merrut link its history to early stone age and Harappan era. Chalk drawings or dark red drawings by primitive men are extensively found in the Vindhyan ranges of Mirzapur district.

Utensils of that age have also been discovered in Atranji-Khera, Kaushambi, Rajghat and Sonkh. Copper articles have been found in Kanpur, Unnao, Mirzapur, Mathura and some other districts. All these finds allude to a civilization prior to the advent of the Aryans in this State. It is most probable that snapped links between the Indus Valley and Vedic civilizations lie buried under the ruins of ancient sites found in this State.

Uttar Pradesh is the rainbow land where the multi-hued Indian Culture has blossomed from times immemorial. Blessed with a variety of geographical land and many cultural diversities, Uttar Pradesh, has been the area of activity of historical heroes like - Rama, Krishna, Buddha, Mahavira, Ashoka, Harsha, Akbar and Mahatma Gandhi. Rich and tranquil expanses of meadows, perennial rivers, dense forestsand fertile soil of Uttar Pradesh have contributed numerous golden chapters to the annals of Indian History. Dotted with various holy shrines and piligrim places, full of joyous festivals, it plays an important role in the politics, education, culture, industry, agriculture and tourism of India.

Garlanded by the Ganga and Yamuna. The two pious rivers of Indian mythology, Uttar Pradesh is surrounded by Bihar in the East, Madhya Pradesh in the South, Rajasthan, Delhi, Himachal Pradesh and Haryana in the west and Uttaranchal in the north and Nepal touch the northern borders of Uttar Pradesh, it assumes strategic importance for Indian defence. Its area of 2,36,286 sq kms. lies between latitude 24 deg to 31 deg and longitude 77 deg to 84 deg East. Area wise it is the fourth largest State of India. In sheer magnitude it is half of the area of France, three times of Portugal, four times of Ireland, seven times of Switzerland, ten times of Belgium and a little bigger than England.

The British East India Company came into contact with the Awadh rulers during the reign of IIIrd Nawab of Awadh. There is no doubt that the history of Uttar Pradesh has run concurrently with the history of the country during and after the British rule, but it is also well-known that the contribution of the people of the State in National Freedom Movement had been significant.

LYRICAL EXPRESSIONS OF BRAJ CULTURE

Sanjhee : This is the colourful art of decorating the ground with flowers. The story goes that Shri Krishna in order to please Radha, decorated the floor with flowers one evening and thereafter this art was known as Sanjhee.

Raaslila : According to the Bhagwat Purana, Shri Krishna along with the gopis had danced the Raas on the banks of the Yamuna at Vrindavan. When the gopis felt conceited about Lord Krishna dancing with them, he disappeared from their midst. In the agony of separation from the beloved Krishna, the gopis recalled and enacted his lilas (divine episodes of his life) which in course of time came to be known as the Raaslila. The Raaslila in its present form is ascribed to Swami Haridas and Shri Narayan Bhatt. Only young Brahmin boys of 13 to 14 years of age can perform the Raaslila. The charming childhood pranks of Shri Krishna constitute the main theme of these dramas.

Charkula : This is a traditional folk dance of Braj, where a female dancer balances a column of lighted lamps over her head while dancing. The charkula, a tapered wooden column with four to five circular tiers has earthen lamps on each level. The number of lamps can range from 51 to 108 at times. The dancer with her face veiled, moves with swift, graceful movements while balancing the 40 to 50 kilogram charkula on her head. A dramatic dance that is visually attractive, it is performed on the Dooj of Holi, to the accompaniment of Rasiya songs rendered by the menfolk.

Rasiya : This is the rich tradition of folk-songs that is found in the Braj area. Rasiya songs describe the love of the divine couple Radha and Shri Krishna. It is an inseparable part of the Holi celebrations and all other festive occasions at Braj. The Rasiya is sung to the rhythm of huge drums, locally known as bumb.

Agra : Once the capital of the Mughals and the city of the Taj Mahal, Agra is just 50 km from Matura. The Taj Mahal, a symphony in white marble, a tribute to eternal love, was built by the Emperor Shah Jahan in memory of his wife Mumtaz Mahal. Other splendid examples of Mughal architecture in Agra include the Agra Fort with its exquisite Pearl Mosque, palaces and darbar halls; the imposing mausoloum of Emperor Akbar at Sikandra, built in an amalgam of Hindu and Muslim architectural styles and Itmad-ud-Daula's tomb, embellished with coloured stone inlay and filigree marble screens.

Fatehpur Sikri : (60 km from Mathura) The wonderful city of Fatehpur Sikri was built by the Emperor Akbar. The marvellously preserved fort, palaces and the tomb of Salim Chishti with its delicate lacy marble screens are worth seeing.

FOLK DANCES OF UTTAR PRADESH

Namagen (Himachal Pradesh): Different regions in Himachal Pradesh have different dances. In most of the dances, men and women dance together in a close formation.

The autumnal hue is celebrated in September by a dance performance called Namagen. The most striking dance amongst these is the Gaddis. The costumes are largely woollen and richly studded ornaments of silver are worn by women.

The dances in Uttar Pradesh range from simple performances to ceremonious ones. They are called the Doms and the Bhotiyas. Among these the Dhurang or Dhuring are related to death ceremonies. These dances aim to free the soul of the dead person from evil spirits. This dance has robust movements and remind one of the hunting dances of Nagas on the eastern borders of India.

Hurka Baul (Uttar Pradesh): The Jhumeila, the Chaunfla of Garhwal and the Hurka Baul of Kumaon are seasonal dances. The Hurka Baul is performed during paddy and maize cultivation. On a fixed day, after the preliminary ritual, the dance is performed in different fields by turns. The name of the dance is derived from hurka, the drum which constitutes the only musical accompaniment, and baul, the song. The singer narrates the story of battles and heroic deeds, the players enter from two opposite sides and enact the stories in a series of crisp movements. The farmers form two rows and move backwards in unison, while responding to the tunes of the song and the rhythm of the players.

A famous dance of Kumaon, Uttar Pradesh, is the Chholiya, performed during marriages. As the procession proceeds to the bride's house, male dancers, armed with swords and shields, dance spiritedly.

Amongst the occupational groups, the most enthusiastic dancers are the dhobis, the chamars and the ahirs. The dhobis dance to celebrate any significant occasion. They sing and dance on the occasion of a birth or marriage, and during Holi or Dussehra. There are Rasa Dances that revolve around the early life of Krishna.

The most interesting group of dances are the dances of the agricultural community which revolve round the annual seasons and which have a ritualistic and a functional dimension.

3

Government and Politics

INTRODUCTION

Uttar Pradesh Legislative Assembly (Vidhan Sabha), the lower house of the bicameral legislature

The state is governed by a parliamentary system of representative democracy. Uttar Pradesh is one of the seven states in India, where the state legislature is bicameral, comprising two houses: the Vidhan Sabha (Legislative Assembly) and the Vidhan Parishad (Legislative Council).The Legislative Assembly consists of 404 members who are elected for five-year terms. The Legislative Council is a permanent body of 100 members with one-third (33 members) retiring every two years. Since Uttar Pradesh sends the largest number of legislators to the national Parliament, it is often considered to be one of the most important states with respect to Indian politics. The state contributes 80 seats to the lower house of the Indian Parliament, Lok Sabha and 31 seats to the upper house of the Indian Parliament, Rajya Sabha.

Uttar Pradesh government is a democratically elected body in India with the Governor as its constitutional head and is appointed by the President of India for a five-year term. The leader of the party or coalition with a majority in the Legislative Assembly is appointed as the Chief Minister by the Governor, and the Council of Ministers are appointed by the Governor on the advice of the Chief Minister. The governor remains a ceremonial head of the state, while the Chief Minister and his council are responsible for day-to-day government functions. The council of ministers consists of Cabinet Ministers and Ministers of State (MoS). The Secretariat headed by the Chief Secretary assists the council of ministers. The Chief Secretary is also the administrative head of the government. Each government department is headed by a Minister, who is assisted by an Additional Chief Secretary or a Principal Secretary, who usually is an officer of Indian Administrative Service, the Additional Chief Secretary/Principal Secretary serve as the administrative head of the department they are assigned to. Each department also has officers of the rank of Secretary, Special Secretary, Joint Secretary etc. assisting the Minister and the Additional Chief Secretary/Principal Secretary.

For purpose of administration, the state is divided into 18 divisions and 75 districts. Divisional Commissioner, an IAS officer is the head of administration on the divisional level. The administration in each district is headed by a District Magistrate, who is an IAS officer and is assisted by a number of officers belonging to state services.

The Uttar Pradesh Police is headed by an IPS officer of the rank of Director General of Police. There are 8 Police Zones, 18 Police Ranges and 75 police districts in the state. An IPS officer in the rank of Additional Director General of Police heads the zones, whereas an IPS officer of the rank of Inspector General of Police or Deputy Inspector General of Policeheads the ranges. A Superintendent of Police, an IPS officer and assisted by the officers of the Uttar Pradesh Police Service, is entrusted with the responsibility of maintaining law and order and related issues in each district.

The judiciary in the state consists of the Allahabad High Court in Allahabad, the Lucknow Bench of Allahabad High Court, district courts and session courts in each district or Sessions Division, and lower courts at the tehsil level. The President of India appoints the chief justice of the High Court of the Uttar Pradesh judiciary on the advice of the Chief Justice of the Supreme Court of India as well as the Governor of Uttar Pradesh. Other judges are appointed by the President of India on the advice of the Chief Justice of the High Court. *Subordinate Judicial Service*, categorized into two divisions viz. Uttar Pradesh civil judicial services and Uttar Pradesh higher judicial service is another vital part of the judiciary of Uttar Pradesh. While the Uttar Pradesh civil judicial services comprise the Civil Judges (Junior Division)/Judicial Magistrates and civil judges (Senior Division)/Chief Judicial Magistrate, the Uttar Pradesh higher judicial service comprises civil and sessions judges. The Subordinate judicial service (viz. The district court of Etawah and the district court of Kanpur Dehat) of the judiciary at Uttar Pradesh is controlled by the District Judge.

Politics in Uttar Pradesh has been dominated by four political parties, the Samajwadi Party, the Bahujan Samaj Party, the Indian National Congress, and the Bharatiya Janata Party. Politicians from Uttar Pradesh have played prominent roles in Union Government of India with some of them having held the high positions of Prime Minister. Uttar Pradesh has been called India's under-achiever because it has provided India with eight prime ministers while remaining a poor state.

GOVERNMENT OF UTTAR PRADESH

The Government of Uttar Pradesh is a democratically elected state government in North Indian state of Uttar Pradesh with the governor as its appointed constitutional head of the state by the President of India. The Governor of Uttar Pradesh is appointed for a period of five years and appoints the chief minister and his or her council of ministers, who are vested with the executive powers of the state. The governor remains a ceremonial head of the state, while the chief minister and his or her council are responsible for day-to-day government functions. The state of Uttar Pradesh's influence on Indian politics is paramount as it sends the largest number of members of parliament to both the Lok Sabha and the Rajya Sabha.

Legislature

The state is governed by a parliamentary system of representative democracy. Uttar Pradesh is one of the seven states in India, where the state legislature is bicameral, comprising two houses: the Vidhan Sabha (legislative assembly) and the Vidhan Parishad (legislative council). The Uttar Pradesh Legislative Assembly consists of 404 members who are elected for five-year terms.

The Uttar Pradesh Legislative Council is a permanent body of 100 members with one-third (33 members) retiring every two years. Since Uttar Pradesh sends the largest number of legislators to the national Parliament, it is often considered to be one of the most important states with respect to Indian politics. The state contributes 80 seats to the lower house of the Parliament of India, the Lok Sabha and 31 seats to the upper house, the Rajya Sabha.

Executive

The government is headed by the governor who appoints the chief minister and his or her council of ministers. The governor is appointed for a period of five years and acts as the constitutional head of the state. The governor remains the ceremonial head of the state with the day-to-day running of the government is taken care of by the chief minister and his or her council of ministers in whom a great deal of legislative powers is vested.

The council of ministers consists of cabinet ministers and ministers of state. The Secretariat headed by the chief secretary assists the council of ministers. The chief secretary is also the administrative head of the government.

Each government department is headed by a Minister, who is assisted by an additional chief secretary or a principal secretary, who usually is an officer of Indian Administrative Service, the additional chief secretary or principal secretary serves as the administrative head of the department they are assigned to. Each department also has officers of the rank of secretary, special secretary, joint secretary etc. assisting the minister and the additional chief secretary or principal secretary.

Administration

Divisional administration

The Indian state of Uttar Pradesh is made up of 75 administrative districts, that are grouped into 18 divisions. Each division consists of 3-7 districts. A divisional commissioner, an officer of the Indian Administrative Service (IAS) is responsible for heading the administration of a division, the Divisional Commissioner is also responsible for the collection of revenue and maintenance of law and order in his or her division.

There are also eight police zones and eighteen police ranges in the state. Each zone consists of 2-3 ranges and is headed by an additional director general-ranked officer of the Indian Police Service (IPS). Whereas a range consists of three to four districts and is headed by an inspector general-ranked or a deputy inspector general-ranked IPS officer.

District administration

A district of an Indian state is an administrative geographical unit, headed by a district magistrate and collector (DM), an IAS officer. The district magistrate is responsible for coordinating the work between various departments in the district, is responsible for law and order in the district and is also given the power of an executive magistrate. The DM is assisted by a number of officers belonging to the Provincial Civil Service and other state services.

A senior superintendent of police or superintendent of police, an IPS officer, is entrusted with the responsibility of maintaining law and order and related issues of the district. He or she is assisted by IPS and Provincial Police Service, in addition to Uttar Pradesh Police officials.

A divisional forest officer, an officer belonging to the Indian Forest Service, in the rank of deputy conservator of forests, is responsible for managing the forests, the environment, and wildlife-related issues of the district with the assistance of the Uttar Pradesh Forest Service.

Sectoral development is looked after by the district head of each development department such as public works, health, education, agriculture, animal husbandry, etc. These officers belong to the various state services. These officers have to report to the DM of the district.

Politics

Uttar Pradesh politics is dominated by the Bharatiya Janata Party, the Samajwadi Party and the Bahujan Samaj Party (BSP) as the third major party. The Bharatiya Janata Party occupies the current government headed by Chief Minister Yogi Adityanath.

VIDHAN

The current chief minister of Uttar Pradesh is Mulayam Singh Yadav, the leader of the Samajwadi Party (Socialist Party). The former Prime Minister of India, Atal Behari Vajpayee, represents the constituency of Lucknow. Unfortunately, the state has been marred by a lot of caste based politics, which has been hindering a sound economic development of the state.

The major political parties in the state are: Samajwadi Party, a Socialist party; Bharatiya Janata Party, a conservative Hindu nationalist party; and the Bahujan Samaj Party, a party whose platform caters to India's untouchable castes, the dalits. No party has received a majority in the state's Assembly since 1991, and the current administration (since 2003) has been held up by smaller parties and independents.

The state has a large number of village councils known as Panchayats just like the other states of India. One of the most developed Panchayats is Shahabad in Maharajganj District of Uttar Pradesh.

Divisions: Agra, Allahabad, Azamgarh, Bareilly, Basti, Chitrakoot, Devipatan, Faizabad, Gorakhpur, Jhansi, Kanpur, Lucknow, Mirzapur, Moradabad, Saharanpur, Varanasi.

Districts: Agra, Aligarh, Allahabad, Ambedkar Nagar, Auraiya, Azamgarh, Badaun, Bagpat, Bahraich, Ballia, Balrampur, Banda, Barabanki, Bareilly, Basti, Bijnor, Bulandshahr, Chandauli, Chitrakoot, Devaria, Etah, Etawah, Faizabad, Farrukhabad, Fatehpur, Firozabad, Gautam Buddha Nagar, Ghaziabad, Ghazipur, Gonda, Gorakhpur, Hamirpur, Hardoi, Jalaun, Jaunpur, Jhansi, Jyotiba Phule Nagar, Kannauj, Kanpur Dehat (Akbarpur), Kanpur Nagar, Kaushambi, Kushinagar (Padrauna), Lakhimpur Kheri, Lalitpur, Lucknow, Mahamaya (Hathras), Maharajganj, Mahoba, Mainpuri, Mathura, Mau, Meerut, Mirzapur, Moradabad, Muzaffarnagar, Pilibhit, Pratapgarh, Raebareli, Rampur, Saharanpur, Sant Kabir Nagar, Sant Ravidas Nagar (Bhadohi), Shahjahanpur, Shravasti, Siddharthnagar, Sitapur, Sonbhadra, Sultanpur, Unnao, Varanasi.

Major Cities: Agra, Allahabad, Kanpur, Lucknow, Meerut, Varanasi.

VIDHAN PARISHAD

The State has a bicameral Legislature since 1937. The Upper House or the Vidhan Parishad is a permanent House. Members are elected or nominated for six years and one-sixth of them retire every second year.

It has 108 members, 12 of whom are nominated by the Governor. Thirty-nine members are elected each by the Vidhan

Sabha and Local bodies and nine each by the teachers and graduates. The Vidhan Parishad has no right to vote on demands for money, nor can any money bill be introduced in it. No other bill can become a law unless passed by both the Hosuse. The presiding officers of Vidhan Parishad are known as Chairman and Deputy Chairman.

They are elected and hold their offices like the presiding officers of Vidhan Sabha. Both the Houses of Legislature have their own separate Secretariats and Secretaries. They function independently of the State Government Secretariat and Secretaries. Both the Secretariats have been divided into sections which look after parliamentary, accounts and committee work.

There is also a library for the use of members of the Legislature. It is the biggest of the Legislature libraries in the country. Members of both the Houses and Committees have the same privileges, powers and immunities as those of the members of the House of Commons in UK. Besides, no prosecution can be launched against them in courts for anything said on the floor of the House.

An important and pioneering contribution made by Uttar Pradesh in the democratic process is the provision of office of the Leader of the Opposition by an Act. Under the new dispensation, he has been given a status at par with that of a minister. He is also given pay equal to that of a minister, and free furnished residence. Provision has also been made for car allowance, staff for his office and other facilities befitting his position. According to the aforesaid Act, the leader of the single largest recognised opposition party, having the strength to make up the quorum, is recognised as the Leader of the Opposition.

DIVISIONS AND DISTRICTS

Uttar Pradesh state consists of seventy districts, which are grouped into seventeen divisions: Agra, Azamgarh, Allahabad, Kanpur, Ghaziabad, Gorakhpur, Chitrakoot, Jhansi, Devipatan, Faizabad, Bahraich, Bareilly, Basti, Mirzapur, Moradabad, Meerut, Lucknow, Varanasi, Farrukhabad and Saharanpur.

CONSTITUENT REGIONS

The state comprises the Doab region (inluding the upper Doab and the lower doab with the Brij bhumi in its centre), which runs along its western border from north to south, the Rohilkhand in the north, Awadh (Oudh) (the historic country of Koshal) in the centre, the northern parts of Bagelkhand and Bundelkhand in the south, and the south-western part of the Bhojpur country, commonly called Purvanchal ("Eastern Province"), in the east.

CONSTITUTIONAL SETUP

Under the Constitution of India, Uttar Pradesh has a Governor and a bicameral Legislature. The Lower House is called Vidhan Sabha and the Upper House, Vidhan Parishad, The State has also a High Court at Allahabad with its bench at Lucknow. The executive power of the State is vested in the Governor as it is exercised by him either directly or through officers subordinate to him according to the constitutional provisions. The Governor is appointed by the President of India and has to be a citizen of India. He/She should not less than 35 years of age.

The Governor holds office at the pleasure of the President. Normally, his term is five years from the date he assumes office. But he can hold office even after the expiry of his term till assumption of office by his successor. The Governor cannot be a member of either of the two Houses of Parliament or any House of the Legislature. He also cannot hold any office of profit and can use his official residence without payment of any rent. Besides, he is also entitled to such pay, allowances and privileges as prescribed by parliament by Law from time to time. In the absence of such a Law he is entitled to such pay, allowances and privileges as specified in the Second Schedule of the Constitution.

COUNCIL OF MINISTERS

There is a Council of Ministers headed by the Chief Minister to aid and advise the Governor in conduct of the business of the government. Barring such matters which are to be decided by the Governor in his discretion under the Law, the Council assists him in all the remaining business. If any question arises as to whether any subject fall within the purview of the Governor's discretionary power, his decision taken in his discretion will be final and cannot be questioned. The Chief Minister is appointed by the Governor who also appoints other ministers on the advice of the Chief Minister.

All the ministers function during the pleasure of the Governor. The Council of Ministers is collectively responsible to the Vidhan Sabha. Before a minister assumes office, he is administered oath of office and secrecy by the Governor as per form prescribed in the Third Schedule of the Constitution. Any minister who does not become a member of the Legislature for six consecutive months ceases to be a minister after the expiry of the six month period. The ministers are entitled to such pay and allowances as may be fixed by the Legislature by law from time to time. They are also entitled to other perquisites, including free furnished residence, & travelling and medical facilities.

All the executive business of the State is carried on in the name of the Governor. The Chief Minister has to inform the Governor about all the decisions taken by the Council of Ministers in regard to administration as also require the Council of Ministers to reconsider any matter on which a unilateral decision has been taken by a minister.

The Governor has been made a component part of the Legislature under Article 168 of the Constitution and has been assigned certain functions. He summons both or either of the Houses of Legislature and also prorogues them. He is also empowered to suspend or dissolve the Vidhan Sabha. He also nominates 12 members to the Vidhan Parishad and one Anglo-Indian member to the Vidhan Sabha. After each general election and thereafter before the commencement of the first session of the Legislature each year, the Governor addresses the joint session of both the Houses and apprises them of the business for whose disposal of which the session of the Legislature has been summoned. He can send messages to any House of the

Legislature in connection with any bill matter pending in it. The House of the Legislature in connection with any ill matter pending in it. The House to which such a message is sent has to consider it as per convenience. The Governor gives assent to the bills passed by the Legislature or may reserve it for the assent of the President. Without assent no bill can become an Act.

Each year the Governor causes the annual financial statement of the concerned year, the report of the Public Service Commission, and the report of the Comptroller and Auditor General of India, pertaining to the accounts of the State, to be laid on the table of both the Houses of the Legislature. He is also empowered to promulgate ordinances when the Legislature is not in session and he is satisfied that the situation requires immediate action. The ordinances thus promulgated have to be placed before the Legislature as soon as it meets and are subject to its approval or disapproval.

POWERS OF THE GOVERNOR

Before assuming office, the Governor is administered an oath by the Chief Justice of the High Court affirming to protect and defend the Constitution and to devote himself to the service and well-being of the people. Under the executive power of the State, the Governor is empowered to grant pardon, reprieve or remission, or to suspend or commute the punishment of any person convicted of any crime against Law.

VIDHAN SABHA

The Uttar Pradesh Vidhan Sabha has a total of 404 members including one Anglo-Indian member who is norminated by the Governor. Till 1967, it had a strength of 431 members including one nominated Anglo-Indian member. According to the recommendation of the Delimitation Commission, which is appointed after every Census, the State had been divided into 403 Vidhan Sabha Constituencies. The Term of the Vidhan Sabha is five years unless dissolved earlier. The election for it is held on the principle of "one adult one vote"

HOUSE COMMITTEES

The House has not enough time to deal with every matter that comes before it or to examine it in detail. So, it works through the Committees. There are committees to deal with Legislation matters like the Select Committee on bills or the Delegated Legislative Committee which examines rules, regulations and by laws framed by the Government underpowers vested in it under the various Acts and the Constitution.

Besides, the House has three important Financial Committees—the Estimates Committee, the Public Accounts Committee, and the Public Undertakings and Corporation Committee. The Estimates Committee examines the estimates presented in the House. The Public Accounts Committee examines the reports of the Comptroller and Auditor-General of India relating to this State and sees to it whether the money spent was actually available or not and had been spent for the purpose for which it was earmarked by the House. Uttar Pradesh is the first State to accept the Principle that the Chairman of Public Accounts Committee should be from the Opposition.

The State has been following this convention since 1948, While it was adopted by the Lok Sabha only after 1967. The Pubic Undertakings and Corporation committee was set up only recently after the setting up of several public sector undertaking in the State. In view of the need for ensuring accountability of public undertakings to the Legislature and the same time preserving their autonomy, the Public Undertaing Committee examines their working and gives them directions so that they may function efficiently, economically and without any unnecessary interference from the Government. Special Committees Besides these Legislative and Financial Committees, there are other committees to assist in the conduct of the business of the House.

The Assurance Committee examines the assurances given by the Government in the House, the Privileges Committee examines cases of violation of privileges raised in the House, while the Petition Committee looks into the petitions submitted to the Vidhan Sabha by the people from time of time. There is another Committee, the House Committee which deals with the boarding and loading facilities of the members.

There is one more important committee of the House, the Business Advisory Committee, which allots and regulates time for business before the House. Uttar Pradesh has also the distinction of setting up of a Parliamentary Studies Committee a few years ago to study parliamentary affairs and give its suggestions.

The committee has done important work regarding privileges of members, ordinance-issuing power of the Governor, inclusion of Vidhan Parishad members in financial and other committees and working of the committee itself. Another committee was set up to oversee the welfare of Scheduled Castes/Tribes and Denotified Tribes. In addition, there are 27 Standing Committees to advise the ministers.

RULES OF THE HOUSE

The Vidhan Sabha has the power to frame rules for regulating and laying down the procedure for the conduct of its business. All the matters coming before the House are decided by a majority vote. The quorum of the House is one-tenth of its membership. The business of the Vidhan Sabha is conducted by the Speaker and in his absence by the Deputy Speaker. Both of these are elected by the members by a majority of votes.

The main business of Vidhan Sabha is to enact laws, grant money for Government expenditure and exercise control over the activities of the Government through debates and raising matters of urgent public importance. The Language of the House is Hindi in Devanagri script. Legislative matters are placed before the House with the permission of the House in the shape of official or non-official bills. After this, the bill is taken up either for consideration of the House directly or referred to a Select or Joint-Select Committee. If the bill is passed after clause by clause consideration by the House, it is sent to the

Vidhan Parishad which may either reject or pass it with amendments. In any case, the Vidhan Sabha may pass the bill with or without amendments.

In case the bill so passed for the second time is rejected or passed with amendments to which the Vidhan Sabha does not agree or is kept pending for a period upto one month by the Vidhan Parishad, the bill is deemed to have been passed by both the Houses of the Legislature and sent to the Governor for his assent. But no money bill can be kept pending by the Vidhan Parishad for more than 14 days from the date of its receipt and if it is kept pending so, it will be deemed as passed by both the Houses and sent to the Governor for his assent. Budget estimates are put to the vote of the House. According to rules, the House can take 5 days for general debate on the estimates and another 24 days for passing them.

The estimates are put before the House for sanction by the ministers on the recommendation of the Governor. They are in shape of demand of grant department-wise. The opposition can move cut motion on these demands. The Constitution has made provision for introduction of proposal for supplementary or additional grants in the House if the expenditure exceeds sanctioned money.

THE SECRETARIAT

Most departments of the Secretariat have heads of departments and heads of offices under their administrative control, who function as the executive authorities of the Government. All the government orders are issued in the name of the Governor but are signed by the Secretary or officers under him down to the rank of nder Secretary.

The work of Government is conducted in Hindi, in Devanagri script. The Principal Secretaries, Secretaries, Special Secretaries, Joint Secretaries, Deputy Secretaries and Under-Secretaries are appointed either from the Central or State Administrative Services. Some Deputy Secretaries and Under Secretaries are also appointed from the permanent Secretariat

Services. As a matter of fact, mostly permanent officers of the Secretariat are appointed to the post of Under Secretary.

Offices in Judical and Legislative Departments are appointed from the Judicial Services. The work of the Secretariat can be divided broadly into the following categories:- (i) Personnel Administration (ii) Financial Administration (iii) Judicial and Legislative Affairs (iv) Law and Order (v) Levy and Collection of Taxes (vi) Economic Development and Conservation of Sources of State's Wealth (viii) Social Services (viii) Public Utility Services (ix) General Administration.

DISTRICT AND DIVISIONAL ADMINISTRATION

After the Secretariat and Heads of Departments, the Divisional Commissioner occupies an important place. He is fully responsible for law and order, revenue, administration and other matters pertaining to his division. He has to exercise supervision over the district officers, local bodies and planning and development works.

Each division consists of certain districts. Each district is under the admistrative charge of a district officer who is also called the District Magistrate or Deputy Commissioner. The District Officer is fully responsible for the law and order in his district and has extensive administrative, police and revenue powers. Besides maintaining revenue records, he has also to look after works relating to planning and development and land reforms. The district is further divided into tehsils, blocks and villages for administrative convenience and for collection of revenue and development works.

THE JUDICIARY

The High Court is the apex court in the State in respect of civil and criminal cases. The Board of Revenue is the highest court in respect of revenue cases. Under Article 277 of the Constitution, the High Court has been given the power of superintendence over all others courts and tribunals. The High

Court is a Court of records which means that its work and proceedings serve as perpetual evidence. Its records are of such high authority that their content cannot be challenged in any lower court.

As a court of record, it has also the power to punish persons guilty of its contempt.

The Chief Justice of the High Court is appointed by the President of India on the advice of the Chief Justice of the Supreme Court of India and the Governor of the State.

Other Judges are appointed by him on the advice of the Chief Justice. Only such persons are eligible for the post of High Court who have worked as an advocate for at least ten years or held office in any Judicial Service for the same period.

The High Court is empowered to issue writs to any person or office for protecting the fundamental rights enshrined in the Constitution. It has both original and appellate jurisdiction in civil as well as criminal cases.

SUBORDINATE JUDICIAL SERVICE

The Subordinate Judiciary has been divided into two parts "The U.P. Civil Judicial Services" and "The U.P. Higher Judicial Service".

The former consists of Munsifs and Civil Judges including Small Cause Judges and the latter of Civil and Sessions Judges (now Additional District Sessions Judges). The District Judge is the controller of the Subordinate Judicial Service at the district level.

The State is divided into 46 judicial districts, each under the control of a District Judge. In certain cases Munsifs and Assistant Collectors and Assistant Session Judge also. The jurisdiction of the District Judge extends to more than one revenue district in some cases. On the civil side, the Munsif's Court is the lowest court. The next higher court is that of the Civil Judge.

The highest court at the district level is that of the District Judge. In criminal cases, the Munsif has the powers of a Judicial

Magistrate. From October 2, 1967, the Judicial Magistrates, who were hitherto under the Government, have been placed under the High Court.

Thus there is now complete separation of judiciary from the executive except for revenue matters. On the revenue side, there are Assistant Collectors. Above them are additional Collectors and Collectors, who have appellate jurisdiction. Higher up are Divisional Commissioner and Additional Commissioners who exercise appellate jurisdiction.

The Board of Revenue is the highest court in revenue matters. Under the Uttar Pradesh Panchayat Raj, Nyaya Panchayats have also been set up. On civil side, they can hear certain cases up to a value or Rs.500. In IPC and other laws. They are not empowered to give prison sentence.

UTTAR PRADESH PUBLIC SERVICE TRIBUNAL

The number of service cases of Government servants in courts was constantly rising. Such cases involved time and money of State Government officers and employees and of State corporations and companies. Keeping this in view, the Uttar Pradesh Public Service Tribunal was set up in 1976 with the objective of rendering speedy and cheaper justice to the employees.

UTTAR PRADESH LEGISLATURE (VIDHAN BHAWAN)

Vidhan Bhawan is located in Lucknow, Uttar Pradesh, India. The state is one of the few in the country which has a bicameral legislature *also called* Vidhan Bhavan with two houses -the lower and the upper. The lower house is the Vidhan Sabha or the *State Legislative Assembly* and the upper house is called the Vidhan Parishad or the *State Legislative council.* The Vidhan Sabha had 431 members till 1967, but now the Vidhan Sabha consists of 403 directly elected members and one nominated member from the Anglo-Indian community. The Vidhan Parishad has 100 members.

Built in 1928, the building was originally called the "Council House" and holds sitting of the legislature of the state of Uttar Pradesh since 1937 along with housing other important offices of Uttar Pradesh Government.

History

In early 20th century, the capital of the state of Uttar Pradesh was Allahabad; a decision was taken in 1922 to move the capital to Lucknow and to construct a building there to house the Assembly Constituency. On 15 December 1922, then Governor of Uttar Pradesh, Spencer Harcourt Butler laid the foundation of the Vidhan Bhawan. The building was designed by Samuel Swinton Jacoband Heera Singh; Singh also drew up the blueprint of the building. Butler subsequently monitored the construction of the building. The building was completed in little over five years at a cost of 21 lakh (US$29,000) (1922 cost not adjusted for inflation) and was inaugurated on 21 February 1928.

Building

Construction of Vidhan Bhawan started 15 December 1922 and took little over five years to complete. The building is made of carvedlight brown sandstone from Mirzapur. Many of the inside halls, galleries and verandas are built of marble from Agra and Jaipur. Circular marble staircases run on both sides of the entrance hall and the walls of the staircases are embellished with paintings. The main chamber of the building is octagonal in shape with circular and dome shaped roof. To house the upper house, construction of the new chamber commenced in 1935 and was completed in 1937. The buildings of both houses (upper & lower) are connected by veranda with offices on both sides.

The sitting of Uttar Pradesh Legislative Assembly is held in the older wing (constructed in 1928) whereas the sittings of the Uttar Pradesh Legislative Council are held in the new wing of the building (constructed in 1937).

Composition of Uttar Pradesh Legislature (Vidhan Bhawan)

Articles 168 to 212 in Part VI of the constitution of India deal with the organisation, composition, duration, officers, procedures, privileges, powers and so on of the state legislature. The Uttar Pradesh Legislature (Vidhan Bhavan) consists of two houses called the Vidhan Sabha and the Vidhan Parishad with the Governor of Uttar Pradesh acting as their head.

Governor of Uttar Pradesh

Articles 153 to 167 in Part VI of the constitution of India deal with the state executive. The state executive consists of the governor, the chief minister, council of ministers and the advocate general of the state. The Governor is the chief executive head of the state. The governor also acts as the agent of the center.

Uttar Pradesh Legislative Assembly (Vidhan Sabha)

The Uttar Pradesh Legislative Assembly is the lower house of the bicameral legislature *(or say Vidhan Sabha is the lower house of Vidhan Bhavan)* of the Indian state of Uttar Pradesh. It has a total of 403 members excluding one Anglo-Indian member who is nominated by the Governor. Till 1967, it had a strength of 431 members including one nominated Anglo-Indian member. According to the recommendation of the Delimitation Commission, which is appointed after every Census, it was revised to 426. After reorganization of the State on 9 November 2000, the strength of the Legislative Assembly has become 404 including one nominated member to represent the Anglo-Indian community. The Term of the Vidhan Sabha is five years unless dissolved earlier. The election is held on the principle of "one adult one vote".

Terms

Every five years new election is done. And new assembly is elected by the people of Uttar Pradesh.

Terms Since 1952

Vidhan Sabha	Constitution	Dissolution	Days
1st	20 May 1952	31 March 1957	1,776
2nd	1 April 1957	6 March 1962	1,800
3rd	7 March 1962	9 March 1967	1,828
4th	10 March 1967	15 April 1968	402
5th	26 February 1969	4 March 1974	1,832
6th	4 March 1974	30 April 1977	1,153
7th	23 June 1977	17 February 1980	969
8th	9 June 1980	10 March 1985	1,735
9th	10 March 1985	29 November 1989	1,725
10th	2 December 1989	4 April 1991	488
11th	22 June 1991	6 December 1992	533
12th	4 December 1993	28 October 1995	693
13th	17 October 1996	7 March 2002	1,967
14th	26 February 2002	13 May 2007	1,902
15th	13 May 2007	9 March 2012	1,762
16th	8 March 2012	11 March 2017	1,829

4

Language and Literature

LANGUAGES

Most people in Uttar Pradesh speak Hindustani, which in a literate form is referred to as Hindi and Urdu.

In addition, the people of Uttar Pradesh speak a variety of local dialects of Hindi, which are not always easy to classify or identify. E.g., the language of Allahabad is often classified today as Awadhi, but, its actually a mix of several surrounding dialects, including Awadhi and Bundelkhandi. Most Allahabadis refer to their dialect as Allahabadi. Furthermore, in neighbouring Banda, the dialect is exactly the same, but, they refer to it as Bundelkhandi.

It's said that in India, the dialects change every 50 mile, and its particularly true of Uttar Pradesh.

The dialect map of Uttar Pradesh is complex, but, in general, in three of the five sub regions of UP, viz, the Doab, Rohilkhand, and Bundelkhand, both Western and Eastern Hindi, as well as a mixture of the two are spoken. E.g., in Upper and parts of lower Doab (till Etawah), various forms of western Hindi are spoken, including Khari boli and Brij Bhasha. In the rest of lower Doab, various mixes of western and Eastern Hindi (Brij

Bhasha/ Bundelkhandi and Awadhi) are spoken). Likewise, in Western Bundelkhand, Bundeli (a language closely related with Brij Bhasha) is spoken, while in Eastern Bundelkhand the dialect is still called 'Bundeli' but is part of Eastern Hindi (actually a mixture of Western and Eastern Hindi). In Western Rohilkhand, Khari boli is spoken. in Central Rohilkhand a mix of Awadhi and Khari boli is spoken, while in Eastern Rohilkhand, Awadhi is the dialect.

In the other two sub-regions of UP, viz., Awadh and Purvanchal too, there exist a wide variation in the dialects spoken. Awadhi is the main dialect in the Awadh sub-region of Uttar Pradesh. But, its form changes from west to east. In western Purvanchal, Eastern Hindi (Awadhi) is spoken, while in districts adjoining Bihar, Bhojpuri, also known as Bihari language is spoken. In southern Purvanchal, Baghelkhandi (a form of Eastern Hindi) is the predominant dialect.

As mentioned earlier, often these dialects merge into each other, for example in Shahjahanpur, in Rohilkhand, Khari boli merges into Awadhi.

Likewise, older districts of Basti, Jaunpur, and western Mirzapur in Purvanchal and Shahjehanpur, Pilbhit, Eastern Badayun and Eastern Farrukhabad in central UP are Awadhi speaking.

Languages of Uttar Pradesh

The languages of Uttar Pradesh generally belong to two zones in the Indo-Aryan languages, Central and East. Hindi is the state's official language (Urdu is co-official), and according to census data, it is spoken by 91.32% of the population. However, Hindi is a wide label that covers many dialects, which may or not be considered separate languages and may or may not be fully mutually intelligible. These include Awadhi, Braj Bhasha, Bundeli, Bagheli, Kannauji, Khariboli (all of these belonging Central zone, considered to be the core of the Hindi belt) and Bhojpuri. Bhojpuri belongs to the Bihari languages of the Eastern zone, and its status as a Hindi language is subject to debate.

History

The languages of Uttar Pradesh mainly derive from the Prakrits of the Old Indo-Aryan languages, and ultimately Sanskrit.

Inventories

Linguists generally distinguish the terms "language" and "dialects" on the basis of 'mutual comprehension'. The Indian census uses two specific classifications in its own unique way: (1) 'language' and (2) 'mother tongue'. The 'mother tongues' are grouped within each 'language'. Many 'mother tongues' so defined would be considered a language rather than a dialect by linguistic standards. This is specifically the case for many 'mother tongues' with tens of millions of speakers that are officially grouped under the 'language' Hindi.

Official languages

The languages of state administration are Hindi, established by the Uttar Pradesh Official Language Act, 1951, and Urdu, established by the Amendment to the same in 1989.

Writing systems

Devanagari is the main script used to write Uttar Pradesh languages, although Urdu is written in the Nastaliq style of the Perso-Arabic script. Kaithi was widely used historically.

The Nagari Pracharini Sabha was formed in 1893 to promote the usage of the Devanagari script.

LITERATURE

Uttar Pradesh has always been rich in languages. The languages that have prevailed in the state are Hindi, Sanskrit, Urdu, Awadhi Braj Bhasha, English, Bhojpuri, Bundeli and Kannauji etc.Uttar Pradesh is the land of famous writers like Kalidas, Tulsidas, Keshavdas and Surdas. The land has seen two of the greatest Sanskrit epics Ramayana and Mahabharata. The prominent locations of literature have been Varanasi, Awadh, and Allahabad.Varanasi, since ancient times, has been the major hub for luminaries to participate in religious and educational debates based on a various range of topics and philosophies.Uttar Pradesh has been the main center for languages like Hindi and Urdu. The state has seen legendary writers and poets like Harivansh Rai Bachchan, Munshi Premchand, Srikant Verma, Mahadevi Verma, Suryakant Tripathi 'Nirala', Sumitra Nandan Pant and Mahavir Prasad Dwivedi etc. Firaq Gorakhpuri, Josh Malihabadi, Akbar Allahabadi, Mazaz Lakhnavi, Kaifi Azmi, Ali Sardar Jafri, Shaqeel Badayuni and Nida Fazili are the names of a few Urdu poets and writers who have contributed towards the rich literature of the state.

LANGUAGE AND LITERATURE

Several texts and hymns of the Vedic literature were composed in Uttar Pradesh. The festival of *Guru Purnima* is dedicated to Sage Vyasa, and also known as *Vyasa Purnima* as it is the day which is believed to be his birthday and also the day he divided the Vedas. There is a long literary and folk Hindi-language tradition in the state. In the 19th and 20th century, Hindi literature was modernised by authors such as Jaishankar Prasad, Maithili Sharan Gupt, Munshi Premchand, Suryakant Tripathi Nirala, Babu Gulabrai, Sachchidananda Hirananda Vatsyayan 'Agyeya', Rahul Sankrityayan, Harivansh Rai Bachchan, Dharamvir Bharati, Subhadra Kumari Chauhan, Mahavir Prasad Dwivedi, Swami Sahajanand Saraswati, Dushyant Kumar, Hazari Prasad Dwivedi, Acharya Kuber Nath Rai, Bharatendu Harishchandra, Kamleshwar Prasad Saxena, Shivmangal Singh Suman, Mahadevi Varma, and Vibhuti Narain Rai. The state is sometimes called the 'Hindi heartland of India'. Hindi became the language of state administration with the Uttar Pradesh Official Language Act of 1951. A 1989 amendment to the act added Urdu, as an additional language of the state. Linguistically, the state spreads across the Central, East-Central, and Eastern zones of the Hindi Belt, the major Hindi dialects of the state being Awadhi, Bhojpuri, Bundeli, Braj Bhasha, Kannauji and the vernacular form of Khariboli.

5

Geography and Flora & Fauna

GEOGRAPHY

Uttar Pradesh, with a total area of 243,290 square kilometres (93,935 sq mi), is India's fourth-largest state in terms of land area and is roughly of same size as United Kingdom. It is situated on the northern spout of India and shares an international boundary with Nepal.

The Himalayas border the state on the north, but the plains that cover most of the state are distinctly different from those high mountains.The larger Gangetic Plain region is in the north; it includes the Ganges-Yamuna Doab, the Ghaghra plains, the Ganges plains and the Terai. The smaller Vindhya Range and plateau region is in the south. It is characterised by hard rock strata and a varied topography of hills, plains, valleys and plateaus.

The Bhabhar tract gives place to the terai area which is covered with tall elephant grass and thick forests interspersed with marshes and swamps. The sluggish rivers of the bhabhar deepen in this area, their course running through a tangled mass of thick undergrowth. The terai runs parallel to the bhabhar in a thin strip. The entire alluvial plain is divided into three sub-regions.The first in the eastern tract consisting of 14 districts which are subject to periodical floods and droughts and have been classified as scarcity areas. These districts have the highest density of population which gives the lowest per capita land. The other two regions, the central and the western are comparatively better with a well-developed irrigation system. They suffer from waterlogging and large-scale user tracts.In addition, the area is fairly arid. The state has more than 32 large and small rivers; of them, the Ganges, Yamuna, Saraswati, Sarayu, Betwa, and Ghaghara are larger and of religious importance in Hinduism.

A part of the Gangetic Plain

Cultivation is intensive. The valley areas have fertile and rich soil. There is intensive cultivation on terraced hill slopes, but irrigation facilities are deficient. The Siwalik Rangewhich forms the southern foothills of the Himalayas, slopes down into a boulder bed called 'bhadhar'. The transitional belt running along the entire length of the state is called the terai and bhabhar area. It has rich forests, cutting across it are innumerable streams which swell into raging torrents during the monsoon.

Physical Features

Uttar Pradesh can be divided into three distinct hypsographical regions:

1. The Himalayan region in the North—Highly rugged and varied terrain; transferred to Uttrakhand. Varying topography; elevation ranges from 300 to 5000m; slope ranges from 150 to 600 m/km.
2. The Gangetic Plain in the centre—Highly fertile alluvial soils; flat topography broken by numerous ponds, lakes and rivers; slope 2 m/km
3. The Vindhya Hills and plateau in the south—Hard rock Strata; varied topography of hills, plains, valleys and plateau; limited water availability.

The Himalayan region comprises the districts of Uttarkashi, Chamoli, Pithorgarh, Tehri-Garhwal, Almora and Nainital tehsil of Nainital District and Chakrata and a part of Dehradun tehsil of Dehradun District. High mountains formed of sedimentary rocks broken by valleys and deep gorges, characterize the terrain. The perpetual snows in the higher reaches are the source of perennial rivers and rivulets which criss-cross the terrain and ultimately find their two rivers together with their tributaries form a big river system which waters the entire Gangetic plain.

The prominent peaks in the hill region include Banarpunch, Mount Kamety, Trishul, Dunagiri, Nanda Devi, Badrinath and Kedarnath. The hill areas are sparsely populated.

There are few trees that can grow in this terrain, and soil is thus subject to heavy erosion. Cultivation is done under intensive soil. Irrigation facilities are deficient and only a small fraction of the total area is under artificial irrigation. The valley areas have fertile and rich soil. There is intensive cultivation on terraced hill slopes. The higher altitudes are suitable for sub-tropical and temperate fruit culture.

The Siwalik Range which forms the southern foothills of the Himalayas, slopes down in to a boulder bed called 'bhadhar'. The transitional belt running along the entire length of the state is called the terai and bhabhar area. It has rich forests, cutting across it are innumerable streams which swell into raging torrents during the monsoon.

The bhabhar tract gives place to the terai area which is covered with tall elephant grass and thick forests interspersed with marshes and swamps. The sluggish rivers of the bhabhar deepen in this area, their course running through a tangled mass of thick under growth. The terai runs parallel to the bhabhar in a thin strip. The main crops are wheat, rice, and sugar cane. Jute also is grown. Tea is grown in the sub mountain area of the Dehradun.

The most important area for the economy of the state is the Gangetic plain which stretches across the entire length of the state from east to west. The entire alluvial plain can be divide into three sub-regions. The first in the eastern tract consisting of 14 districts which are subject to periodical floods and droughts and have been classified as scarcity areas. These districts have the highest density of population which gives the lowest per capita land.

The other two regions, the central and the western are comparatively better with a well-developed irrigation system. They suffer from water logging and large-scale user tracts. The Gangetic plain is watered by the Jamuna, the Ganga and its major tributaries, the Ramganga, the Gomati, the Ghaghra and Gandak. The whole plain is alluvial and very fertile. The chief crops cultivated here are rice, wheat, millets, gram, and barley. Sugar cane is the chief cash crop of the region.

The Southern fringe of the Gangetic is demarcated by the Vindhya Hills and plateau. It comprises the four districts of Jhansi, Jalaun, Banda, and Hamirpur in Bundelkhand division, Meja and Karchhana tehsils of Allahabad district, the whole of Mirzapur District south of Ganga and Chakia tehsil of Varanasi District. The ground is strong with low hills. The

Betwa and Ken rivers join the Jamuna from the south-west in this region. It has four distinct kinds of soil, two of which are agriculturally difficult to manage. They are black cotton soil. Rainfall is scanty and erratic and water-resources are scare. Dry farming is practical on a large scale.

Uttar Pradesh is the most populous state in India and the fourth largest in terms of area. It has to its north, Tibet and Nepal, to its north-west, Himachal Pradesh, to its west, Haryana, to its south-west, Rajasthan and Madhya Pradesh, to its south Madhya Pradesh and to its east Bihar.

Many holy rivers of India like the Ganga, the Yamuna, Saryu, Gomti, Rapti, Gandaki and Betravati run through this state. Several sacred places associated with India's rich heritage like, Badrinath, Kedarnath, Haridwar, Ayodhya, Mathura, Vrindavan, Kashi and Prayag are also located in this state.

Climate

Monsoon clouds over Lucknow

Uttar Pradesh has a humid subtropical climate and experiences four seasons. The winter in January and February is followed by summer between March and May and the monsoon season between June and September.

Summers are extreme with temperatures fluctuating anywhere between 0 °C and 50 °C in parts of the state coupled with dry hot winds called the *Loo*. The Gangetic plain varies from semiarid to sub-humid.

The mean annual rainfall ranges from 650 mm in the southwest corner of the state to 1000 mm in the eastern and southeastern parts of the state. Primarily a summer phenomenon, the Bay of Bengal branch of the Indian monsoon is the major bearer of rain in most parts of state. After summer it is the south-west monsoon which brings most of the rain here, while in winters rain due to the *western disturbances* and north-east monsoon also contribute small quantities towards the overall precipitation of the state.

Anandabodhi tree in Jetavana Monastery, Sravasti

*A hybrid nasturtium (***Tropaeolum majus***) showing nectar spur, found mainly in Hardoi district*

The rain in UP can vary from an annual average of 170 cm in hilly areas to 84 cm in Western U.P. Given the concentration of most of this rainfall in the four months of the monsoon, excess rain can lead to floods and shortage to droughts. As such, these two phenomena, floods and droughts, commonly recur in the state. The climate of the Vindhya Range and plateau is subtropical with a mean annual rainfall between 1000 and 1200 mm, most of which comes during the monsoon. Typical summer months are from March to June, with maximum temperatures ranging from 30 to 38 °C (86 to 100 °F). There is low relative humidity of around 20% and dust-laden winds blow throughout the season. In summers, hot winds called *loo* blow all across Uttar Pradesh.

FORESTS

Near the snow line there are forests of rhododendrons and betula (bhojpatra). Below them are forests of silver fir, spruce, deodar, chir and oak. On the foothills and in the terai-bhabhar area grow the sal and gigantic haldu. Along river courses the shisham grows in abundance. The Vindhyan forests have dhak, teak, mahua, salai, chironji and tendu. The hill forests also have a large variety of medicinal herbs.

Sal, chir, deodar and sain yield building timber and railway sleepers. Chir also yield resin, the chief source of resin and turpentine. Sisso is mostly used for furniture while khair yields kattha, which is taken with betel leaves or pan. Semal and gutel are used as matchwood and kanju in the plywood industry. Babul provides the principal tanning material of the state.

Some of the grasses such as baib and bamboo are raw material for the paper industry. Tendu leaves are used in making bidis (Indian cigarettes), and cane is used in baskets and furniture.

Species of grasses have been collected from the Gangetic plain. Herbs include medicinal plants like Rauwolfia serpentina, Viala serpens, podophyllum, hexandrum and Ephecra gerardiana.

ANIMAL LIFE

Corresponding to its variegated topography and climate, the state has a wealth of animal life. Its avifauna is among the richest in the country. Animals that can be found in the jungles of Uttar Pradesh include the tiger, leopard, wild bear, sloth bear, chital, sambhar, jackal, porcupine, jungle cat, hare, squirrel, monitor lizards, and fox. These can be seen in all but the highest mountain ranges. The most common birds include the crow, pigeon, dove, jungle fowl, black partridge, house sparrow, peafowl, blue jay, parakeet, kite, mynah, quail, bulbul, kingfisher and woodpecker.

Certain species are found in special habitats. The elephant is confined to the terai and the foothills. The gond and para also found in this region. The chinkara and the sandgrouse prefer a dry climate, and are native to the Vindhyan forests. The musk deer and the brown bear is found in the higher Himalayas. Among the game birds resident in the state are the snipe, comb duck, grey duck, cotton teal and whistling teal.

Several species of wildlife have become extinct in Uttar Pradesh. Among them are the lion from the Gangetic plain and the rhinoceros from the terai. The fate of many species is uncertain, including the tiger, black buck, serow, musk deer, swamp deer, bustard, pink-headed duck, chir and mural pheasants and four-horned antelope. Although a determined enforcement of laws against poaching and hunting has yielded some results, the wildlife population today is alarmingly low. Gharials are poached for their skin.

To preserve its wild life the state has established one National Park; Corbett National Park and 12 game sanctuaries. The Corbett National Park is situated partly in Ramnagar and partly in the Kalagarh forest division. It is one of the showpieces of the state

GEOGRAPHY AND LOCATION

Uttar Pradesh is India's fourth largest and most populous [States of India], located in the north-central part of the country. It spreads over a large area, and the plains of the state are quite distinctly different from the high mountains in the north. The climate of this state can also vary widely - primarily due to it being far from the moderating effect of the sea and the occasional cold air arising due to western disturbances - with temperatures reaching as high as 49 °C in summer, and as low as -1 °C in winter.

Location

Uttar Pradesh is bounded by Uttarakhand and Himachal Pradesh on the north-west, Haryana and Delhi on the west, Rajasthan on the south-west, Madhya Pradesh on the south, Chhattisgarh and Jharkhand on south-east and Bihar on the east. Situated between 23°52'N and 31°28'N latitudes and 77°3' and 84°39'E longitudes, this is the fourth largest state in the country in terms of area, and the first in terms of population. Uttar Pradesh can be divided into three distinct hypsographical regions :

1. The Shivalik foothills and Terai in the North
2. The Gangetic Plain in the centre - Highly fertile alluvial soils; flat topography broken by numerous ponds, lakes and rivers; slope 2 m/km
3. The Vindhya Hills and plateau in the south - Hard rock Strata; varied topography of hills, plains, valleys and plateau; limited water availability.

The Shivalik Range which forms the southern foothills of the

Himalayas, slopes down into a boulder bed called Bhabhar, The transitional belt running along the entire length of the state is called the Terai and bhabhar area.

It has rich forests, cutting across it are innumerable streams which swell into raging torrents during the monsoon. The bhabhar tract gives place to the terai area which is covered with tall elephant grass and thick forests interspersed with marshes and swamps. The sluggish rivers of the bhabhar deepen in this area, their course running through a tangled mass of thick under growth.

The terai runs parallel to the bhabhar in a thin strip. The main crops are wheat, rice, and sugar cane. Jute also is grown. The most important area for the economy of the state is the Gangetic plain which stretches across the entire length of the state from east to west. The entire alluvial plain can be divide into three sub-regions.

The first is the eastern tract consisting of 14 districts which are subject to periodical floods and droughts and have been classified as scarcity areas. These districts have the highest density of population which gives the lowest per capita land. The other two regions, the central and the western are comparatively better with a well-developed irrigation system. They suffer from water logging and large-scale user tracts. The Gangetic plain is watered by the Yamuna, the Ganges and its major tributaries, the Ramganga, the Gomati, the Ghaghra and Gandak.

The whole plain is alluvial and very fertile. The chief crops cultivated here are rice, wheat, pearl millet, gram, and barley. Sugar cane is the chief cash crop of the region. The southern fringe of the Gangetic is demarcated by the Vindhya Hills and plateau. It comprises the four districts of Jhansi, Jalaun, Banda, and Hamirpur in Bundelkhand division, Meja and Karchhana tehsils of Allahabad district, the whole of Mirzapur district south of Ganges and Chakia tehsil of Varanasi district. The ground is strong with low hills. The Betwa and Ken rivers join the Yamuna from the south-west in this region. It has four distinct kinds of soil, two of which are agriculturally difficult to manage. They are black cotton soil. Rainfall is scanty and erratic and water-resources are scarce. Dry farming is practical on a large scale.

Climate

The climate of the state is tropical monsoon. The average temperature varies in the plains from 3 to 4 °C in January to 43 to 45 °C in May and June. There are three distinct seasons - winter from October to February, summer from March to mid-June, and the rainy season from June to September.

The rain fall in the plains is heaviest in the east and decreases towards the north-west. Floods are a recurring problem in the state, causing damage to crops, life and property. The worst floods were in 1971, when 51 of the 54 districts of the state were affected — an area of nearly 52,000 square kilometres. The eastern districts are the most vulnerable to floods, the western districts slightly less and the central region markedly less. The eastern districts susceptibility to floods is ascribed, among other things, to heavy rainfall, low flat country, high subsoil water level and the silting of beds which causes river levels to rise. The problem in the western districts is mainly poor drainage caused by the obstruction of roads, railways, canals, new built-up areas etc. There is water logging in the large areas. The major flood-prone rivers are the Ganges, Yamuna, Gomti, Ghaghara, Rapti, Sharda and Ramganga. The inadequate drainage capacity of the smaller western Sirsa, Kali and the Aligarh drain is also a cause of floods.

Flora and fauna

Recorded Forest Area constitute about 6.88% of the total geographical area of the state and Total Forest and Tree cover is 9.01% of total geographical area. The terai and bhabhar area in the Gangetic Plain have most of the forests. The Vindhyan forests consists mostly of scrub. The districts of Jaunpur, Ghazipur and Ballia have no forest land, while 31 other district have less forest area.

CLIMATE OF UTTAR PRADESH

The climate of Uttar Pradesh (U.P.) is primarily defined as *humid subtropical with dry winter* (CWa) type with parts of Western U.P. as *semi-arid* (BS) type. Alternatively, some authors refer to it as *tropical monsoon.* Variations do exist in different parts of the large state, however the uniformity of the vast Indo-Gangetic Plain forming bulk of the state gives a predominantly single climatic pattern to the state with minor regional variations. U.P. has a climate of extremes. With temperatures fluctuating anywhere from 0 °C to 50 °C in several parts of the state and cyclical droughts and floods due to unpredictable rains, the summers are extremely hot, winters cold and rainy season can be either very wet or very dry.

Seasons of Uttar Pradesh

Indian Meteorological Department (IMD) breakdowns the climate of India into the following seasons:

1. Winter Season / Cold Weather Season (January and February)
2. Summer season/ Pre-monsoon season/ Hot weather season/ Thunderstorm season (March, April and May)
3. South-west Monsoon/ Summer Monsoon (June, July, August and September)
4. Post-monsoon or Northeast monsoon or Retreating SW Monsoon season (October, November and December)

This classification is primarily Monsoon centric given the vast effect that it casts on the lives and agriculture of India.

Classification of the Uttar Pradesh climate

The climate of Uttar Pradesh is generally defined to be *tropical monsoon type.* However based on the Köppen climate classification, it can be classified mostly as *Humid Subtropical with dry winter (CWa) type* with parts of Western U.P. as *Semi-Arid (BS) type* (refer to map of India above)

Based on IMD classification, UP has the following three predominant seasons:

1. Winter Season - November to February
2. Summer season - March, April and May
3. South-west Monsoon - June, July, August, September and October

Retreating Monsoon season, although existent, has a very negligible effect in Uttar Pradesh and only occasional mild showers are experienced in winter. Some of these showers are not even due to the Monsoon but due to western disturbances.

The primary temperature, rainfall and wind features of the three Distinct Seasons of U.P. can be summarized as below:

1. Summer (March–June): Hot & dry (temperatures rise to 45 °C, sometimes 47-48 °C); low relative humidity (20%); dust laden winds.
2. Monsoon (June–September): 85% of average annual rainfall of 990 mm. Fall in temperature 40-45° on rainy days.
3. Winter (October–February): Cold (temperatures drop to 3-4 °C, sometimes below -1 °C); clear skies; foggy conditions in some tracts.

Given significant climatic differences, U.P. has been divided into two meteorological sub-divisions - U.P. East and U.P. West.

Geographical terrain

The state of Uttar Pradesh is in the heart of Indo-Gangetic Plain with River Ganges flowing right through it, Himalayas to the north of it and the Chota Nagpur Plateau and the Vindhyas to the south of it.

Temperature

Temperature varies from 0 to 46 °Cs. High temperatures of around 50 °C have been recorded in Gonda district of U.P. Given such a wide range of temperature fluctuations in most parts of the state, it can lead to either cold waves or heat waves both resulting in substantial loss of life and economy.

Heat waves

In 2007, Banda with 45.5 °C temperature was the leader in terms of hot districts of U.P. for several days. At least 62, people were reportedly dead during the heat wave that year.In June 2009, 30 people died of heatstroke in U.P. Highest temperatures reached 49 °C in Bundelkhand district of northern U.P. In June 2010, Jhansi recorded the highest temperature of 46.7 °C, the hottest for U.P. for that year.

Cold waves

In recent years, winters at the end of 2007 and beginning of year 2008 caused a string of cold-wave related deaths in U.P. with temperatures as low as 2.8 °C in the city of Meerut, U.P. Simultaneously it also led to a loss of crops and agricultural produce. Similarly last part of 2009, saw the mercury-dipping to lows of 2.9 °C in Meerut again causing loss of human life. End of 2010 and starting of 2011 was no different with winters bringing news of cold-wave related deaths. This time Churk town in Sonabhadra district ranked coldest with 1.4 °C.

Precipitation

It rains over most of U.P. with very few arid or semi-arid patches. Snowfall doesn't occur but hail-storms, frost and dew occur often in U.P. The type of rainfall that U.P. receives is orographic, cyclonic and convectional.

Rain

Primarily a summer phenomenon, the Bay of Bengal branch of the Indian Monsoon is the major bearer of rain in most parts of U.P. It is the South-West Monsoon which brings most of the rain here, although rain due to the *western disturbances* and North-East Monsoon also contribute small quantities towards the overall precipitation of the state. The rain in U.P. can vary from an annual average of 170 cm in hilly areas to 84 cm in Western U.P. Given the concentration of most of this rainfall in the 4 months of Monsoon period, excess rain can lead to floods and shortage to droughts. As such these two phenomenons of floods and droughts are a common recurrence in the state.

Floods in U.P.

Floods are a known hazard of U.P. due to overflowing of its main rivers like Ganga, Yamuna, Ramganga, Gomti, Sharda, Ghaghra, Rapti and Gandak. Estimated annual losses due to floods in U.P. is 4.32 billion (US$60 million).

Major flood management efforts have been undertaken to mitigate the risk. Most of these floods occur due to the Monsoon rains and overflowing of rivers during the rainy periods. Year 2010 witnessed one such year of flooding in U.P.

Droughts in Uttar Pradesh

Shortage of rain during the highly variable Monsoon season can cause droughts in U.P. leading to severe loss to man and property. Recent 2002 and 2004 drought related financial estimates have been reported to be 75.4 billion (US$1.1 billion) and 72.92 billion (US$1.0 billion). The recurrence of a major deficiency in annual rainfall follows a 6–8 years cycle in Eastern U.P. whereas in Western U.P., it is a 10 years cycle.

Wind

In summers, hot winds called *loo* blow all across U.P. They are dust-laden and quite damaging. In winters, dry and rainless winds blow across the state. Fog may also form in parts of U.P.

PILIBHIT TIGER RESERVE

Pilibhit Tiger Reserve is located in Pilibhit district, Lakhimpur Kheri District and Bahraich District of Uttar Pradesh state in India. It lies along the India-Nepal border in the foothills of the Himalayas and the plains of the 'terai' in Uttar Pradesh. It is one of India's 41 Project Tiger Tiger reserves.

Pilibhit is one of the few well forested districts in Uttar Pradesh. According to an estimate of year 2004, Pilibhit district has over 800 km (310 sq mi) forests, constituting roughly 23%

of the district's total area. Forests in Pilibhit have at least 36 tigers and a good prey base for their survival.

History

With Corbett Tiger Reserve going to Uttrakhand, Uttar Pradesh always wanted to develop the Pilibhit forests area as a home for the striped cats. A proposal, created in 2005, to make a home for the endangered cats in Pilibhit forests was sent to the government of India in April 2008. Pilibhit Tiger Reserve was declared in September 2008 on the basis of its special type of ecosystem with vast open spaces and sufficient feed for the elegant predators.

Geography

The northeastern boundary of the reserve is the River Sharda (Nepali:Mahakali River) which defines the Indo-Nepal border, while the southwest boundary is marked by the River Sharda and the River Ghaghara. The reserve has a core zone area of 602.79 km(232.74 sq mi) and buffer zone area of 127.45 km (49.21 sq mi). Elevation ranges from 168 to 175 meters above MSL

Flora

This reserve is one of the finest examples of the highly diversified and productive Terai-Duar savanna and grasslands eco-system. The Terai forests and grasslands constitute habitat for over 127 animals, 556 bird species and 2,100 flowering plants. They are also home to around 6 million people who depend on them for their livelihoods.

Fauna

Pilibhit Tiger Reserve is home to a large number of rare and threatened species, which include Bengal tiger, Indian leopard, swamp deer, hispid hare and Bengal floricans.

The *Dudhwa tigers* are distributed in one major and three smaller populations. Major population is constituted by Dudhwa reserve which includes Dudhwa National Park, Kishenpur and Katarniaghat wildlife sanctuaries, Pilibhit forests and north and south Kheriforests. Smaller tiger populations are present in Bijnor forests in west and Suhelwa and Sohagibarwa wildlife sanctuaries in east.

According to a study by Wildlife Institute of India (WII), the Dudhwa-Pilibhit tiger population has high conservation value since it is the only population having the ecological and behavioural adaptations of the tiger unique to the Tarai region.

FLORA AND FAUNA

View of the Terai region

Gharial (**Gavialis gangeticus**) *is found in the Ganges river*

The state has an abundance of natural resources. In 2011 the recorded forest area in the state was 16,583 km (6,403 sq mi) which is about 6.88% of the state's geographical area. In spite of rapid deforestation and poaching of wildlife, a diverse flora and fauna continue to exist in the state. Several species of trees, large and small mammals, reptiles, and insects are found in the belt of temperate upper mountainous forests.

Medicinal plants are found in the wild and are also grown in plantations. The Terai-Duar savanna and grasslands support cattle. Moist deciduous trees grow in the upper Gangetic plain, especially along its riverbanks. This plain supports a wide variety of plants and animals. The Ganges and its tributaries are the habitat of large and small reptiles, amphibians, fresh-water fish, and crabs. Scrubland trees such as the babool and animals such as the chinkara are found in the arid Vindhyas.

Tropical dry deciduous forests are found in all parts of the plains. Since much sunlight reaches the ground, shrubs and grasses are also abundant. Large tracts of these forests have been cleared for cultivation. Tropical thorny forests, consisting of widely scattered thorny trees, mainly babool are mostly found in the southwestern parts of the state. These forests are confined to areas which have low annual rainfall (50–70 cm), a mean annual temperature of 25–27 °C and low humidity.

Uttar Pradesh is known for its extensive avifauna. The most common birds which are found in the state are doves, peafowl, junglefowl, black partridges, house sparrows, songbirds, blue jays, parakeets, quails, bulbuls, comb ducks, kingfishers, woodpeckers, snipes, and parrots. Bird sanctuaries in the state include Bakhira Sanctuary, National Chambal Sanctuary, Chandra Prabha Sanctuary, Hastinapur Sanctuary, Kaimoor Sanctuary, and Okhla Sanctuary.

Other animals in the state include reptiles such as lizards, cobras, kraits, and gharials. Among the wide variety of fishes, the most common ones are mahaseer and trout. Some animal species in Uttar Pradesh have gone extinct in recent years, while others, like the lion from the Gangetic Plain and the rhinoceros from the Terai region, have become endangered. Many species are vulnerable to poaching despite regulation by the government.

Uttar Pradesh: Flora and Fauna

Uttar Pradesh has plenty of natural resources. Diverse flora and fauna exist in state despite of indiscriminate deforestation and poaching. In the belt of temperate mountainous forests, species of reptiles, insects, mammals and trees are found.

Common birds which are found in Uttar Pradesh are sparrows, parakeets, songbirds, quails, kingfishers, woodpeckers, blue jays, comb ducks, parrots, snipes, black partridge, peacocks, junglefowl, doves, bulbuls and house sparrows. Due to the availability of sunlight, shrubs, herbs and grasses are also abundant in the state.

Large and small species of fauna survive in the Ganges as well as in its tributaries. In 2011, the forest area in Uttar Pradesh was recorded to be 16,583 km2. It is about 6.88 per cent of the geographical area of the state. The famous Bird sanctuaries in Uttar Pradesh are National Chambal Sanctuary, Hastinapur Sanctuary, Bakhira Sanctuary, Chandra Prabha Sanctuary, Okhla Sanctuary and Kaimoor Sanctuary.

The upper Gangetic plain is known for the growth of moist deciduous trees. Tropical thorny forests along with thorny trees are found in the south western parts of Uttar Pradesh. Reptiles in the state include cobras, lizards, ghariyals and kraits. Some animals in the state have become extinct and some are in the verge of extinction. Some of the common fishes in the state are trout and mahaseer.

DIVISIONS, DISTRICTS AND CITIES

Uttar Pradesh is divided into 75 districts under these 18 divisions:

1. Saharanpur
2. Moradabad
3. Bareilly
4. Lucknow
5. Devipatan
6. Basti
7. Gorakhpur
8. Meerut
10. Aligarh

11. Agra
12. Kanpur
13. Faizabad
14. Azamgarh
15. Jhansi
16. Chitrakoot
17. Prayagraj
18. Varanasi
19. Mirzapur

Divisions of Uttar Pradesh

Each district is governed by a District Magistrate, who is an Indian Administrative Serviceofficer appointed Government of Uttar Pradesh and reports to Divisional Commissioner of the division in which his district falls.

The Divisional Commissioner is an IAS officer of high seniority. Each district is divided into subdivisions, governed by a sub-divisional magistrate, and again into Blocks. Blocks consists of panchayats (village councils) and town municipalities. These blocks consists of urban units viz. census towns and rural units called gram panchayat.

Uttar Pradesh has more metropolitan cities than any other state in India. The absolute urban population of the state is 44.4 million, which constitutes 11.8% of the total urban population of India, the second-highest of any state. According to the 2011 census, there are 15 urban agglomerations with a population greater than 500,000. There are 14 Municipal Corporations, while Noida and Greater Noida in Gautam Budh Nagar district are specially administered by statutory authorities under the *Uttar Pradesh Industrial Development Act, 1976.*

In 2011, state's cabinet ministers headed by the then Chief Minister Mayawati announced the separation of Uttar Pradesh into four different states of Purvanchal, Bundelkhand, Avadh Pradesh and Paschim Pradesh with twenty-eight, seven, twenty-three and seventeen districts, respectively, later the proposal was turned down when Akhilesh Yadav lead Samajwadi Party came to power in the 2012 election.

UTTAR PRADESH WILDLIFE

Nestling in the foothills of Himalayas, Uttar Pradesh has been an abode to the rare species of the world. The state has many wildlife sanctuaries and various national parks.

Visit the most famous Corbett National Park gifted with a varied topography and vegetation. The park has the highest density of Tiger in the country. View the wild animals in their natural habitat.

Rajaji National Park possesses as many as 23 species of mammals and 315 birds' species. Nanda Devi National Park in Garwhal Himalaya offers a delightful combination of flora and fauna. Other places of interest are Valley of flowers, Kaimoor Wildlife Sanctuary, Ranipur Wildlife Sanctuary, Dudwa National Park and so on.

Chandra Prabha Wildlife Sanctuary

Location: Near Varanasi (Uttar Pradesh)

Area: 78 sq. kms.

Main Species: Panther, Chinkara.

Best Season: Mid-November to Mid-June

Established in 1997, Chandra Prabha Sanctuary, a small sanctuary sprawling over an area of 78 sq. kms, is located on Naugarh and Vijaigarh hillocks in Vindhya forest range, in Chandauli district. The sanctuary, rich in varied types of flora and fauna is a feast to the eyes and a perfect treat for the nature lover.

The Wildlife Population: The sanctuary has a rich and varied wildlife, which comprises of panther, chinkara, sambar, chital, partridge and peafowl. Leopard, hyena, jackal, wolf and 'sehi' bear can be seen roaming around in the tranquil environs of the park.

The park is a bird watchers' paradise, as one can see around

150 species of birds. The wild vegetation comprises mahua, saagun, amaltas, tendu, koraiya, ber etc.

Hastinapur Wildlife Sanctuary

Location: Meerut, Ghaziabad (Uttar Pradesh)

Area: 2073 sq. kms.

Year Of Establishment: 1986

Main Species : 1986

Founded in 1986, in Meerut, Ghaziabad, Bijnore and Jyotiba Phule Nagar, The Hastinapur Sanctuary sprawling in an area of 2073 sq. kms, is inhabited by varied types of wild animals like the swamp deer, chital, nilgai, wolf, leopard, hyena, gharial and wild boar.

The Wild Popualtion: The population of the wild animals includes various species of animals including antelope, sambhar, cheetal, blue bull, leopard, hyena, wild cat, and different types of birds. It also houses alligators.

Kaimoor Wildlife Sanctuary

Location: Uttar Pradesh-Bihar Border

Established In: 1982

Main Species: Antelope, Blue Bull, Leopard

Time To Visit: November To April

Kaimoor sanctuary, located on the Uttar Pradesh - Bihar border, is spread over an area of 500 sq. km. The sanctuary, established in 1982 is easily accessible by road. The wildlife population comprises leopard, blackbuck, chital, chinkara, ratel and peafowl.

The Wildlife Population: The main species of wild animals found in the sanctuary are those of antelope, blue bull, wild cat, karakal, and bijju. There are quite a few varieties of local & migratory birds forming a large part of the wild population.

Important Vegetation includes saal, sheesham teek, mahua, jamun, siddha, salai, koraiya and jheengar.

Mahavir Swami Wildlife Sanctuary

Location: Lalitpur (Uttar Pradesh).

Main Species: Leopard, Neel Gai

Area: 5.4 sq. kms.

Established in: 1977

Located in Lalitpur in Uttar Pradesh, the Mahavir Wildlife Sanctuary is spread over an area of 5.4 sq. km. The sanctuary is 125 km from Jhansi, the magnificent gateway to the Bundelkhand region, rendered famous by the legendary Rani Laxmi Bai.

Some of the key attractions of the sanctuary are the leopard, neelgai, wild boar, and sambhar.

Wild Population: The main population of the sanctuary consists of animals such as leopard, neel gai, wild boar and sambhar and there is a rich variety of avian population. The region is also very rich in flora

National Chambal Wildlife Sanctuary

Location: Etawah, Agra (Uttar Pradesh)

Established in: 1979

Area: 635 sq. kms.

Species: Crocodile, Alligator

The National Chambal Sanctuary, located in Etawah, near Agra is spread over an area of 635 sq. kms. Established in 1979, the park has a rare collection of exotic rarely found species. The unusual gangetic dolphin is the main attraction of National Chambal sanctuary. The sanctuary is presently a part of a large area co-administered by Rajasthan, Madhya Pradesh and Uttar Pradesh.

Wild Population: The main attraction of the sanctuary is the rare gangetic dolphin. The park is inhabited by crocodiles, alligators, chinkara, sambhar, nilgai, wolf and wild boar. There are also a large number of terrestrial and aquatic animals.

Nawabganj Bird Sanctuary

Location: 45 Kms From Lucknow (Uttar Pradesh)

Established In: Woodpecker, Parakeet

Best Season: Throughout The Year

Nawabganj bird sanctuary, located 45 kms from Lucknow is Home to several migratory and water birds.

An ideal site for bird watching and photography, this sanctuary has a huge marshland and shallow lake bordered with mixed dry forest. The avian population of the sanctuary comprises among others the pochard, shoveller, woodpecker, parakeet, coot, purple moorhen and common teal.

Wild Population: Nawab ganj sanctuary is rich in avian population. It has a good number of avian population including pochard, shoveller, woodpecker, parakeet, coot, purple moorhen and common teal.

Ranipur Wildlife Sanctuary

Location: Uttar Pradesh

Area: 230 sq.kms

Altitude: 259 mrs. average

Main Species: Leopard, Tiger, Chinkara

This 230 sq. kms.of sanctuary is rich in wildlife. It is the natural habitat of many animals including leopard, tiger, sloth bear, sambar, blackbuck, peafowl, spur-fowl, jungle fowl, printed partridge, fishing cat and chinkara.

6

Economy

ECONOMY OF UTTAR PRADESH

In terms of net state domestic product (NSDP), Uttar Pradesh is the second-largest economy in India after Maharashtra, with an estimated gross state domestic product of 14.89 lakh crore(US$210 billion), and hence contributes 8.406% of India. Agriculture is the leading occupation in Uttar Pradesh.

According to the report generated by India Brand Equity Foundation (IBEF), in 2014–15, Uttar Pradesh has accounted for 19% share in the country's total food grain output. The state has experienced a high rate of economic growth in the past few years. Food grain production in the state in 2014–15 stood at 47,773.4 thousand tonnes. Wheat is the state's principal food crop and sugarcane is the main commercial crop particularly in Western Uttar Pradesh. About 70% of India's sugar comes from Uttar Pradesh. Sugarcane is the most important cash crop as the state is country's largest producer of Sugar. As per the report generated by Indian Sugar Mills Association (ISMA), total sugarcane production in India was estimated to be 28.3 million tonnes in the fiscal ending September 2015 which includes 10.47 million tonnes from Maharashtra and 7.35 million tonnes from Uttar Pradesh.

Located in the rich fertile Indo-Gangetic Plain, Agriculture is the largest employment generator in the state.

Net State Domestic Product at Factor Cost at Current Prices (2011–12 Base) figures in crores of Indian Rupees

Year	Net State Domestic Product
2011-12	229,074
2012-13	256,699
2013-14	294,031
2014-15	332,352
2015-16	384,718
2016-17	453,020
2017-18	1,446,000 crore(US$200 billion) (est.)

State industries are localised in the Kanpur region, the fertile purvanchal lands and the Noida region. The Mughalsarai is home to a number of major locomotive plants. Major manufacturing products include engineering products, electronics, electrical equipment, cables, steel, leather, textiles, jewellery, frigates, automobiles, railway coaches, and wagons. Meerut is sports capital of India and also a jewelry hub. More small-scale industrial units are situated in Uttar Pradesh than in any other state, with 12 per cent of over 2.3 million units. With 359 manufacturing clusters, cement is the top sector of SMEs in UP.

Varanasi's Dashashwamedh Ghat; Tourism is important sector of Uttar Pradesh economy and holy cities of Varanasi, Mathura and Ayodhya attracts pilgrims from all over the world.

The Uttar Pradesh Financial Corporation (UPFC) was established in the year 1954 under the SFCs Act of 1951 mainly to develop small- and medium-scale industries in the state. The UPFC also provides working capital to existing units with a sound track record and to new units under a single window scheme. As of July 2012, due to financial constraints and directions from the state government, lending activities have been suspended except for State Government Schemes. The state has reported total private investment worth over Rs. 25,081 crores during the years of 2012 and 2016. According to a recent report of World Bank on Ease of Doing Business in India, Uttar Pradesh was ranked among the top 10 states and first among Northern states.

In 2009–10, the tertiary sector of the economy (service industries) was the largest contributor to the gross domestic product of the state, contributing 44.8% of the state domestic product compared to 44% from the primary sector (agriculture, forestry, and tourism) and 11.2% from the secondary sector (industrial and manufacturing). MSME sector is the second-largest employment generator in Uttar Pradesh, the first being agriculture and employs over 92 lakh people across the state. Under the leadership of Akhilesh Yadav, Uttar Pradesh has exceeded 11 five-year plan targets and has established several Micro Small and Medium Enterprises (MSMEs) and generated 6.5 lakh employment opportunities across the state.[1] During the 11th five-year plan (2007–2012), the average gross state domestic product(GSDP) growth rate was 7.28%, lower than 15.5%, the average for all states of the country. The state's per capita GSDP was 29,417 (US$410), lower than the national per capita GSDP of 60,972 (US$850). The state's total financial debt stood at 2,000 billion (US$28 billion) in 2011. Labour efficiency is higher at an index of 26 than the national average of 25. The economy also benefits from the state's tourism industry.

The state is attracting foreign direct investment which has mostly come in the software and electronics fields; Noida and Lucknow are becoming major hubs for the information technology (IT) industry and house the headquarters of most of the major corporate, media and financial institutions. Sonebhadra, a district in eastern Uttar Pradesh, has large-scale industries. Its southern region is known as the *Energy Capital of India*. In May 2013 Uttar Pradesh had the largest number of mobile subscribers in the country, a total of 121.60 million mobile phone connections out of 861.66 million in India, according to the telecom regulator, Telecom Regulatory Authority of India (TRAI).

Economy

The economy of Uttar Pradesh is the fourth largest of all the states of India. According to the state budget for 2017-18,

Uttar Pradesh's gross state domestic product is 16.89 lakh crore (US$240 billion). The largest Indian state, Maharashtra, has an urban population of 50,818,259, while Uttar Pradesh has an urban population of 44,495,063. According to the 2011 census report, 22.3% of Uttar Pradesh's population lives in urban areas. The state has 7 cities with populations exceeding 1 million each. After partition in 2000, the new Uttar Pradesh state produces about 92% of the economic output of the old Uttar Pradesh state. In 2011, the Tendulkar committee reported that 29.43% of Uttar Pradesh's population is poor, while the Rangarajan committee reported that 39.8% of the population is poor.

In the tenth five-year planning period of 2002 and 2007, Uttar Pradesh registered an annual economic growth rate of 5.2%. In the eleventh period, between 2007 and 2012, Uttar Pradesh registered an annual economic growth rate of 7%. In 2012-13 and 2013–14, however, the growth rate decreased to 5.9% and 5.1%, respectively, one of the lowest in India. The state's debt was estimated at 67% of the gross domestic product in 2005. In 2012, the state was one of the highest receivers of overall remittances to India which stood at $0.1 billion (Rs. 3,42,884.05 crore), along with Kerala, Tamil Nadu, and Punjab.Additionally, the state government has selected five cities for Metro train projects: Meerut, Agra, Kanpur, Lucknow, and Varanasi. The Lucknow Metro project was completed in September of 2017. Uttar Pradesh is an agrarian state, and it contributed 8.89% in food grain production to the country in 2013-14.

Agriculture, livestock and fishing

Uttar Pradesh is a major contributor to the national food grain stock. In 2013-14, this state produced 50.05 million tones of foodgrain, which is 18.90% of the country's total production. This is partly due to the fertile regions of the Indo-Gangetic plain and partly due to irrigation facilities such as canals and tube-wells. Lakhimpur Kheri is a densely populated sugar-producing district in the country. It has been the most common producer of food grains in India since the 1950s, due to high-yielding varieties of seed, greater availability of fertilizers and increased use of irrigation. Western Uttar Pradesh is more advanced in terms of agriculture as compared to the other regions in the state. The majority of the state's population depends upon farming activities. Wheat, rice, pulses, oilseeds and potatoes are major agricultural products. Sugarcane is the most important cash crop throughout the state. Uttar Pradesh is one of the most important states in India as far as horticulture is concerned. Mangoes are also produced in the state.

Uttar Pradesh supports about 15% of India's total livestock population. In 1961, its livestock comprised 15% cattle, 21% buffaloes, 13% goats, and 8% other livestock. Between 1951 and 1956 there was an overall increase of 14% in the livestock population. There are about 8,000 km^2 of water area, including lakes, tanks, rivers, canals, and streams. The fishing area in the state is over 2,000 km^2 and there are more than 175 varieties of fish.

Industry

UP has witnessed rapid industrialization in the recent past, particularly after the launch of policies of economic liberalization in the country. As of March 1996, there were 1,661 medium and large industrial undertakings and 296,338 small industrial units employing 1.83 million persons. The per capita state domestic product was estimated at Rs 7,263 in 1997–98 and there has been a visible decline in poverty in the state. However, nearly 40 percent of the total population lives below the poverty line.

There are numerous types of minerals in the state and many industries have come up based on these minerals. There are a number of cement plants in Mirzapur in the Vindhya region, a bauxite-based aluminium plant in the Banda region and Sonbhadra region. In the hilly regions of the state, many non-metallic minerals are found which are used as industrial raw materials. Coal deposits are found in the Singrauli region. Nevertheless, the state is poor in mineral resources. The only considerable deposits are of limestone in Mirzapur district. These are being extracted and are used largely in cement manufacture.

Uttar Pradesh has a booming electronics industry, especially in the UP-Delhi-NCR and Lucknow-Kanpur Corridors where many electronics units are produced.

Cottage industries, such as handloom and handicrafts, have traditionally provided livelihood to a large number of people in the state. These industries include:

- Varanasi is a world-famous centre of handloom woven, embroidered textiles; the main products are Zari-embroidery and brocade-work on silk sarees. Lucknow is a centre of 'Chikan' embroidery, renowned for its grace and delicacy, a skill more than 200 years old. Uttar Pradesh produces about 15% of the total fabric production of the country, employs about 30% of the total workforce of artisans in India and is responsible for an annual production of about $0.1 million USD in the state.
- Varanasi is well known for manufacturing the diesel-electric locomotives at Diesel Locomotive Works. The workshop at DLW is further upgraded to manufacture electric locomotives for Indian Railways. It is the largest diesel-electric locomotives manufacturer in India.
- The state has two major production centres of leather and leather products, with over 11,500 units; Agra and Kanpur are the key centres. About 200 tanneries are located in Kanpur.
- Moradabad is renowned for brass work and has carved a niche for itself in the handicraft industry throughout the world. Lately, other products that are produced here like iron sheet metalwares, aluminium artworks, wood works and glasswares have become popular with the numerous foreign buyers, and are therefore being exported in large quantities. On an average Moradabad exports goods worth Rs. 30–40 billion each year, which constitutes 40% of total exports from India under this category.
- Meerut is one of the biggest gold market in Asia. It is one of the largest exporter of sports related items and music instruments of the country.

- Bulandshahr is renowned for Khurja Pottery worldwide. There are nearly 23 export oriented units and they are exported to foreign countries such as the United Kingdom, USA, Australia, New Zealand, United Arab Emirates, and others. The Sikandrabad industrial area, developed by UPSIDC, has a large number of national and multinational companies working here successfully.

Minerals and heavy industries

Uttar Pradesh has ample reserves of coal, dolomite, and gems. Other important minerals include diaspore, sulphur, magnesite, pyrophyllite, silica sand and limestone. Ghaziabad, Gautam Buddh Nagar, Kanpur, Lucknow, Faizabad, Sonbhadra, Mirzapur, and Balrampur are the most industrious areas in the state.

Mathura Refinery situated in Mathura is the only oil refinery in Uttar Pradesh, and is the 6th largest oil refinery in India.

Handloom and handicrafts

Handlooms and handicrafts are a very important source of income in UP. There are thousands of power looms and handlooms in the state, most of which are situated in eastern UP. Many people depend on it for their livelihood. Main centres in eastern UP include Tanda, Banaras, Azamgarh, Bhadohi, Mau and Mau Aima. In western UP some of the important centres are Meerut and Etawah. In eastern UP, Tanda is a small town with a population of approximately 150,000 people with over 100,000 power looms. The main products include Lungis, Gamchas, Stoles, Arabic Rumaal, and garment clothes.

Services

The service industry plays a large role in the economy of Uttar Pradesh. It contributed nearly 49% of the gross state domestic product in 2017-18. Uttar Pradesh is the 'IT-Hub' of North India, with a share of software exports next to that of Karnataka. But unlike South Indian states, IT enterprises are limited to particular areas only, such as Noida, Greater Noidaand

Ghaziabad, which lie in the National Capital Region (NCR) and in the state capital Lucknow.

Noida is also famous for TV News broadcasters. Almost all News channels such as ABP News, Zee News, NDTV and Mahua News are located in Film City.

Infrastructure

The infrastructure condition in UP pales in comparison to the other advanced states of India. In 2013, the central government declared the construction of Chaudhary Charan Singh International Airport in Lucknow and Lal Bahadur Shastri Airport in Varanasi. In January 2015, it was announced that the Metro Train project for Lucknow would be completed as of December 2016. The Uttar Pradesh government bus service is one of the largest in the country with more than 10,000 buses. The length of national highway and railway track is highest in Uttar Pradesh in India. A new international airport had been proposed in Kushinagar district. Uttar Pradesh has the most number of national highways. The Yamuna Expressway which is between New Delhi to Agra, is one of the best highways of the country. In 2015, the state government started another expressway project between Agra to Lucknow which will reduce the journey time, it was inaugurated on 21 November 2016. On 31 December 2015, Prime Minister Narendra Modi announced an expressway between New Delhi and Meerut, which will cost 7500 crore. It will reduce the journey time to one hour.

Natural resources

Uttar Pradesh is divided into three natural regions: Bhabar and Terai, the plain of the Ganga and the Yamuna rivers, and the southern plateau. Important minerals include diaspore, sulfur and magnesite, pyrophyllite, silica sand and limestone.

Education

Uttar Pradesh has one of the lowest literacy rates among

Indian states. With just 69.72% literacy rate, UP is ranked 29th in India according to the 2011 census.

TRANSPORTATION

Lucknow Swarna Shatabdi Express near New Delhi.

Inside view of the new airport terminal building

The state has the largest railway network in the country but in relative terms has only sixth-highest railway density despite its plain topography and largest population. As of 2011, there were 8,546 km (5,310 mi) of rail in the state. Allahabad is the headquarters of the North Central Railway and Gorakhpur is the headquarters of the North Eastern Railway. Other than Zonal Headquarters of Allahabad and Gorakhpur, Lucknow and Moradabad serve as divisional Headquarters of the Northern Railway Division. Lucknow Swarna Shatabdi Express, the second fastest shatabdi train, connects the Indian capital of New Delhi to Lucknow. This was the first train in India to get the new German LHB coaches. The railway stations of Lucknow NR,

Kanpur Central, Varanasi Junction, Agra Cantt, Gorakhpur Junction, Mathura Junction included in the Indian Railways list of 50 world-class railway stations.

New Yamuna Bridge in Allahabad is part of National Highway 30

The state has a large, multimodal transportation system with the largest road network in the country. The state is well connected to its nine neighbouring states and almost all other parts of India through the national highways (NH). It boasts 42 national highways, with a total length of 4,942 km (9.6% of the total NH length in India). The Uttar Pradesh State Road Transport Corporation was established in 1972 to provide economical, reliable, and comfortable transportation in the state with connecting services to adjoining states and boasts as being the only State Transport Corporation that runs in profit in the entire nation. All cities are connected to state highways, and all district headquarters are being connected with four lane roads which carry traffic between major centres within the state. One of them is Agra Lucknow Expressway, which is a 302 km (188 mi) controlled-access highway constructed by Uttar Pradesh Expressways Industrial Development Authority (UPEIDA) to reduce vehicular traffic in previously congested roads. This expressway is country's largest Greenfield Expressway which reduced the travel time between Lucknow and Agra from 6 hours to 3.30 hours. Other district roads and village roads provide villages accessibility to meet their social needs as also the means to transport agriculture produce from village to nearby markets. Major district roads provide a secondary function of linking between main roads and rural roads. Uttar Pradesh has the highest road density in India, (1,027 km per 1000 km) and the largest surfaced urban-road network in the country (50,721 km).

The state has two international airports located in Lucknow (Chaudhary Charan Singh International Airport) and Lal Bahadur Shastri International Airport in Varanasi. and four domestic airports located at Agra, Allahabad, Gorakhpur and Kanpur. The Lucknow Airport is the second-busiest airport in North India after the Indira Gandhi International Airport, New Delhi. The state has also proposed creating the Taj International Airport at Kurikupa near Hirangaon, Tundla in Firozabad district. Two more international airports have been proposed to be built at Kushinagar and Jewar, Greater Noida. TheLucknow Metro, is being constructed in the city of Lucknow, and Kanpur Metro as an alternative mode of transport. The capital cities are witnessing a swift rise in the number of immigrants and this has called for the transformation of Public modes of transport.

AGRICULTURE

The western region of the state is more advanced in terms of agriculture. Majority of the population depends upon farming as its main occupation. Wheat, rice, sugar cane, pulses, oil seeds and potatoes are its main products. Sugar cane is an important cash crop almost through out the state and sugar mills and other cane crushers who produce gur and Khandsari are common throughout the state. Uttar Pradesh is an important state in so far as horticulture is concerned. Apples and mangoes are produced in the state.

INDUSTRIES

There are different types of minerals and several industries have came up based on the minerals. There are cement plants in the Mirzapur area in the Vindhya region, a bauxite based aluminium plant in the Banda area and copper in Pithora Garh, Almora Chamboli and Tehri Garhwal. In the hills a number of minerals are to be found, mainly non-metallic minerals which are used as industrial raw materials. Coal deposits are found in the Singrauli area. The industries include a large printing establishment units engaged in manufacturing of scales, locks, letter boxes, furniture, badges and belts, leather goods, scissors etc. Handloom, carpet, glass, electrical goods, electro plating, building material industries are also found in the city.

MINERAL RESOURCES

The state is poor in mineral resources. The only considerable deposits are of limestone in Mirzapur, Dehra Dun and Almora districts. These are being quarried and are used largely in cement manufacture.

Dolomite occurs in small quantities in Bandal and Varanasi districts, gypsum in Tehri Garhwal, Nainital and Dehra Dun districts, andalusite in Mirzapur district, magnetite in Almora and Pithoragarh districts, pyrophyllite and diaspore in Jhansi and Hamirpur districts, phosphorite in the Musoorie area and bauxite in Karvi tehsil of Banda district and in southern part of Varanasi district.

The occurrence of stibnite, a source of antimony has been reported from Chamoli district. At Singrauli in Mirzapur district coalfield is located.

LIVESTOCK AND FISHERY

Uttar Pradesh supports about 15% of the country's total livestock population. Of its livestock in 1961, 15% were cattle, 21% buffaloes, 13% goats and 8% other livestock. Between 1951 and 1956 there was an overall increase of 14% in the livestock population. There are nearly eight lakh hectares of water area, including lakes, tanks, rivers, canals and streams.

The fishing area is over two lakh hectares and more than 175 varieties of fish, excluding the sornamental varieties are found. Among them are rohu, hilsa, mahseer, mangar, snow trout and mirror carp Uttar Pradesh is a very fertile region and a major contributor to the national foodgrain stock. It is also home to 78% of national livestock population. This is a chart of output of major commodities of Uttar Pradesh.

Commodity	*National Share*
Potato	47%
Sugarcane	45%
Wheat	38%
Groundnut	34%
Molasses	34%
Sugar	30%
Tobacco	20%

Industry: Over 3% of the S&P CNX 500 conglomerates have corporate offices in Uttar Pradesh.

Macro-economic Trend: This is a chart of trend of gross state domestic product of Uttar Pradesh at market prices estimated by Ministry of Statistics and Programme Implementation with figures in millions of Indian Rupees.

Year	*Gross State Domestic Product*
1980	155,540
1985	277,480
1990	555,060
1995	1,062,490
2000	1,730,680

Uttar Pradesh's gross state domestic product for 2004 is $1.2 trillion in current prices. After partition, the new Uttar Pradesh state produces about 92% of the output of the old Uttar Pradesh state. Uttar Pradesh is the second largest economy in India after Maharashtra. Under the ambitious policy of Mulayam Singh, Chief Minister, Uttar Pradesh has emerged a robust industrial and agriculture centre. It one of the eight states in India that have been chosen for FDI. In the fiscal year 2005-2006 it received an investment of $124.67 billion.

7

Tourism

TOURISM IN UTTAR PRADESH

Uttar Pradesh ranks first in domestic tourist arrivals among all states of India with more than 71 million, owing to its rich and varied topography, vibrant culture, festivals, monuments, ancient places of worship, and viharas. Uttar Pradesh is also home to three World Heritage Sites: the Taj Mahal, Agra Fort, and the nearby Fatehpur Sikri.

Millions gather at Allahabad to take part in the Magh Mela festival on the banks of the Ganges. This festival is organised on a larger scale every 12th year and is called the Kumbh Mela, where over 10 million Hindu pilgrims congregate in one of the largest gatherings of people in the world.

The historically important towns of Sarnath and Kushinagar are near to Gorakhpur and are located not far from Varanasi. Gautama Buddha gave his first sermon after his enlightenment at Sarnath and died at Kushinagar; both are important pilgrimage sites for Buddhists. Also at Sarnath are the Pillars of Ashoka and the Lion Capital of Ashoka, both important archaeological artefacts with national significance. At a distance of 80 km from Varanasi, Ghazipur is famous not only for its Ghats on the Ganges but also for the tomb of Lord Cornwallis, the 18th-century Governor of East India Company ruled Bengal

Presidency. The tomb is maintained by the Archaeological Survey of India. The state also has a bird sanctuary in Etah district called Patna Bird Sanctuary.

Lucknow, the capital of the state, has several beautiful historical monuments.

Kumbh Mela 2013 at Sangam, Allahabad

To promote tourism, the Directorate of Tourism was established in the 1972 with a Director General who is an IAS. officer. In 1974 the Uttar Pradesh State Tourism Development Corporation was established to look after the commercial tourist activities.

IMPORTANT OF TOURISM PLACES

Situated in the northern part of India, bordering with the capital of India New Delhi, Uttar Pradesh is one of the most popular and an established tourist destination for both Indians and non-Indians alike in India. The most populous state of India, Uttar Pradesh contains a large number of historical monuments and places of religious significance. Geographically, Uttar Pradesh is very diverse, with Himalayan foothills in the extreme north and the Gangetic Plain in the centre. It is also home of India's most visited sites, the Taj Mahal, and Hinduism's holiest city, Varanasi.

Taj Mahal, one of the most famous tourist destinations in Uttar Pradesh and India.

Kathak, one of the eight forms of Indian classical dances, originated from Uttar Pradesh. Uttar Pradesh is at the heart of India, hence it is also known as *The Heartland of India.* Cuisine of Uttar Pradesh like Awadhi cuisine, Mughlai cuisine, Kumauni cuisine are very famous not only in India but also many places abroad.

Uttar Pradesh is known for its rich culture and tradition. It is home to Ayodhya and Mathura birthplace of Lord Rama and Lord Krishnarespectively. Uttar Pradesh attracts a large number of both national and international tourists. Taj Mahal, one of the New Seven Wonders of the World in Agra is also located in Uttar Pradesh.

There are different places one can visit in Uttar Pradesh. Agra, Jhansi, Lucknow and Meerut are historical cities famous for their monuments.

Mathura, Vrindavan, Gokul, Varanasi, Ayodhya and Allahabad are holy cities for Hindus and Kushinar and Sarnath are important Buddhistplaces among the main four pilgrimage sites related to the life of Gautama Buddha. Noida is the most developed urban city of Uttar Pradesh.

To boost the tourism in the state from within the country and other parts of the world, the Government of Uttar Pradesh established a 'Uttar Pradesh Heritage Arc' covering the cities of Agra, Lucknow and Varanasi.

Agra

The 17th-century Taj Mahal in Agra is the most popular monument in India, attracting over 7 million visitors per year. Agra is home to four World Heritage Sites in Taj Mahal, Agra Fort, Sikandra & the Fatehpur Sikri. Agra is also home to many other Mughal buildings like Akbar's Tomb, Itmad-Ud-Daulah etc. Dayal Bagh is an under-construction temple that many visit. The lifelike carving in marble is not seen anywhere else in India.

Kumbh Mela

Every year thousands gather at Allahabad to take part in the festival on the banks of the Ganges, the Magh Mela. The same festival is organised in a larger scale every 12th year and attracts millions of people and is called the Kumbha Mela. Kumbh Mela (especially the Maha Kumbh Mela) is the most sacred of all the pilgrimages. Thousands of holy men and women (monks, saints and sadhus) attend, and the auspiciousness of the festival is in part attributable to this. The sadhus are seen clad in saffron sheets with plenty of ashes and powder dabbed on their skin per the requirements of ancient traditions. Some called *nanga sanyasis* or 'Dhigambers' may often be seen without any clothes even in severe winter, generally considered to live an extreme lifestyle. This tends to attract a lot of western attention as it is seemingly in contrast to a generally conservative social modesty practised in the country.

A procession of Akharas marching over a makeshift bridge over the Ganges river, Kumbh Mela at Allahabad, 2001

Hindu religious sites

Millions of tourists and pilgrims visit the cities of Prayagraj, Varanasi, Mathura, Soron, and Ayodhya, as those are considered to be the holiest cities in India.

Varanasi

Varanasi (also called Kashi and Benares) is widely considered to be the oldest city in the world, before Jerusalem. It is famous for its ghats (steps along the river) which are populated year round with people who want to take a dip in the holy Ganges River.

Kashi Vishwanath Temple in Varanasi is home to the Vishwanath Jyotirling temple, which is one of the most sacred of Hindu Temples.

Varanasi attracts thousands of Hindu pilgrims every year.

Mathura-Vrindavan

Birthplace of Lord Krishana. Both Mathura & Vrindavan have temples devoted to Krishna. During Holi, a special form of Holi called the Lath mar Holi is played here.

Janmaashtami, the birth of Lord Krishna, is celebrated in the region.

Ayodhya

Hindus believe the birthplace of Lord Rama to be in Ayodhya at the place called Ram Janmabhoomi, the site of the demolished Babri Mosque.

Ayodhya is also the birthplace of five Tirthankars, including the first Tirthankar of Jainism, Shri Rishabh Dev. He is known as the father of Jain religion. The city is also important in the history and heritage of Buddhism in India, with several Buddhist temples, monuments and centers of learning having been established here during the age of the Mauryan Empireand the Gupta Dynasty. Ayodhya reached its glorious peak as known to history during the reign of the Guptas over India.

Swaminarayan led the Swaminarayan Sampraday sect of Hinduism and lived here during his childhood years. It was from Ayodhya that Swaminarayan started his seven-year journey across India as Neelkanth.

Tulsidas is said to have begun the writing of his famous Ramayana poem Shri Ramacharitamanas in Ayodhya in 1574 CE. Several Tamil Alwar mention the city of Ayodhya. Ayodhya is also said to be the birthplace of Bahubali, Brahmi, Sundari, King Dasaratha, Acharya Padaliptasurisvarji, King Harishchandra, Shri Rama, Achalbhrata, and the ninth Gandhara of Mahavir Swami.

The Atharva Veda called Ayodhya "a city built by gods and being as prosperous as paradise itself".

Soron Shukar Kshetra is salvation land of Lord Varah and birthland of Sant Tulsidas.

Buddhist religious sites

Uttar Pradesh has many sites which are connected to Lord Buddha and hence, are sacred to Buddhist.

- Sarnath: a place where he held his first public discourse. Also at Sarnath is the Ashoka Pillar with the Lion Capital, is important archaeological artifact with national significance.
- Kushinagar: Where he attained Mahaparinirvana (Demise).
- Kaushambi: Where Buddha delivered many sermons.
- Sankassa: Where he descended after addressing his mother in Heaven.
- Sravasti: His favorite monsoon resort.

Jain religious sites

Parshvanatha, the twenty-third tirthankara, was born in *Benaras* (now Varanasi) in 872 BCE. According to Jain tradition, Kashi (now *Varanasi*) is the birthplace of three more tithankaras, namely Suparshvanatha, Chandraprabha and Shreyansanatha.

According to Jain tradition, five *tirthankaras* were born at Ayodhya, including Rishabhanatha, Ajitanatha, Abhinandananatha, Sumatinatha and Anantanatha. Uttar Pradesh has many sites which are connected to Jainism and hence, are sacred to Jains.

- Hastinapur : This is a popular religious site since it is believed to be birthplace of three Tirthankar Shantinatha, Kunthunath and Aranatha.
- Deogarh, Uttar Pradesh : There are 31 Jain temples built inside fort belonging to 8th-9th century.
- Sarnath : Sarnath is believed to be birthplace of Shreyansnath.
- Bada Gaon
- Bundelkhand :

Bundelkhand, in the heart of India, has been an ancient centre of Jainism. It is mostly in modern Madhya Pradesh, but part of it is in Uttar Pradesh.

Places of interest

Places of interest in Uttar Pradesh include:

- Varanasi – The origin of Hinduism and the oldest city of the world, also known as *City of temples*, holy place for devotees of Lord Shiva, one of the finest Textiles Industry in the world.
- Agra – Taj Mahal and several others historical monuments and gardens.
- Allahabad or Prayag – Well known for its Kumbh Mela. The place where Indian national river Ganges and Yamuna and Saraswati rivers meet. A mass Hindu pilgrimage in which Hindus gather at the Ganges river. Akbar forts, one of the most popular religious center of ancient and modern India for Hinduism. Uttar Pradesh's administrative and education capital.
- Kanpur – Uttar Pradesh's commercial and Industrial hub, several historical places from Mughal, British era.

- Kanpur Sangrahalaya, a museum
- Lucknow – The capital of Uttar Pradesh, Several historical places Mughal, British and ancient India.
- Mathura-The birthplace of Lord Krishna of Hinduism and Neminath of Jainism.
- Vrindavan
- Ayodhya – The birthplace of Lord Vishnu's incarnation prabhu Shri Rama.
- Jhansi – Historical place, Rani Lakshmibai's battlefield against British, Jhansi Fort.
- Bareilly — A large city of Uttar Pradesh with many attractions such as Bake Bihari Ttemple, Hari Temple, Ala Hazrat, and Gandhi Udhayan. The *jhumka* style of music is associated with Bareilly.
- Sarnath-Gautama Buddha first taught the Dharma, the Buddha as one of the four places of pilgrimage which his devout followers should visit. The birthplace of Shreyansanath, the eleventh Jain Tirthankar of the Jainism.
- Kushinagar – It is an important Buddhist pilgrimage site, where Gautama Buddha is believed to have attained Parinirvana after his death.
- Fatehpur Sikri-Historical place for Mughal Empire's palaces and forts.

A panoramic view of the Fatehpur Sikri Palace, Uttar Pradesh

- Meerut – The historical place of the Sepoy Mutiny of 1857 or the First War of Indian Independence. Indian Historical place from Mahabharata period of ancient India to Modern Uttar Pradesh, India.
- Mirzapur Division – A hub of carpet Industries, and popular tourist destination for its natural environment and one of the fastest growing region of Uttar Pradesh.
- Ghaziabad – Historical places from ancient India to modern India and India's fastest growing Industrial city .
- Noida and Greater Noida – IT, Electronics and education hub of Northern India.India's biggest city with planned and iconic skyscrapers.
- Gorakhpur – The city was home to Buddhist, Hindu, Muslim, Jain and Sikh saints. The birthplace of Paramhansa Yogananda, great Hindu emperor Chandragupta Maurya Gorakhpur is also famous for Gorakshanath Temple (Gorakhnath Math), Chauri Chaura, Gita press, Gita Vatika, Ramgarh Tal Lake
- Jaunpur – Historical city founded by the Sultan of Delhi, Feroz Shah Tughlaq and named in memory of his father, Muhammad bin Tughluq as Jaunpur Sultanate. Mughals, Lodis and Islamic forts.
- Dudhwa National Park – Dudhwa Tiger Reserve, Birds Sanctuary, the unique Frog Temple at Oyal, Surat Bhawan Palace, Elephant Rides.
- Rehar – Several major tourist attractions can be mentioned in the town's surroundings, like Jim Corbett National Park (India) about 24 km, Nainital (India) about 69 km
- Gonda - Mulagandhakuti. The remains of Buddha's hut in Jetavana Monastery, Sravasti in Gonda Division and Swaminarayan Chhapaiyâ: The village of Chhapaiya is situated at a distance of 50 km from the district headquarters. The chief interest of the place is Swaminarayan temple which marks the birthplace of

Swaminarayan, or Sahajanand Swami, who was born here on 2 April 1781 as Ghanshyam Pande. Ghanshyam left Chhapaiya at the age of 11 to travel to the pilgrimage sites around India. He completed his pilgrimage in Western Gujarat, where he assumed the leadership of Swaminarayan Sampradaya. The Akshardham temples in New Delhi and in Gandhinagar, Gujarat built by his spiritual successor, Pramukh Swami Maharaj, are both dedicated to him. His followers consider him to be a manifestation of the Supreme Godhead.[10] There have been many movies about the Swaminarayan filmed in this temple in Chhapaiya and in nearby places in the district.

TOURISM PLACES

Western UP: Hastinapur (Meerut), Vrindavana (Mathura), Mathura, Garhmukteshwara (Ghaziabad), Agra, Fathepur Sikri (Agra), Peeran Kaliyar (Sahranpur), Golagokarannath (Kheri), Sankissa, Kannauj, Kampil (Farrukhabad), Soron (Etah), Naimisharanya, Chakratirtha (Sitapur), Shukratal (Muzaffaranagar), Bithur (Kanpur), Lucknow, Deva Sharif (Barabanki).

Eastern UP: Gorakhnath Temple (Gorakhpur), Sarnath (Varanasi), Saidpur Bhitri (Ghazipur), Shringverpur (Allahabad), Kaushambi, Chunar, Vindhyachala (Mirzapur), Devipatan (Gonda), Magahar (Basti), Bhrigu Temple (Ballia), Shravasti, Ayodhya (Faizabad), Kushinagar, Chitrakut, Jaunpur etc.

Keeping ample and abundant prospects of tourism in the State in view, it has been declared an industry by the Government for providing basic tourist facilities to the people, developing tourist spots and earning foreign exchange.

Budhist Circuit : This includes Sarnath, Piparhwa, Samhita, Shrawasti and Kaushambi.

Bundelkhand Region : This includes all the tourist spots of the Jhansi Division.

AGRA

The Ganga Ma (Mother Ganga), the sacred river flow through this state. The water of Ganga is believed to have a purifying effect on the soul. India's holiest city Varanasi is on the banks of this sacred river. It is India's fourth largest state with an area of 2,94,413 sq km.

This city is 200 Km away from Delhi. Agra flourished under the Mughal emperor Akbar (1542-1605) and his successors, Jahangir and Shah Jahan. The destinations given below provide an insight into the range of India's culture and history. It encompass some of the country's most spectacular architecture.

Taj Mahal : The Taj Mahal is situated at Agra, about 200 Kms away from Delhi on the banks of the river Yamuna. It is at Taj Road, Open from 0800 to 1600, Tuesday to Sunday. Taj Mahal is the enduring monument of love. It is a mausoleum. Shajahan build it on the death of his beloved wife Arjumand Bonu Begam (Mumthaz Mahal).

The unique beauty of Taj makes it one of the wonders of the world. It is build with white marble. It was studded with precious stones. (crystal from China, Lapis Lawzuli from Afghanistan and Ceylon, Turquoise from Tibet, Gold from Egypt, amethyst from Persia, agate from Yeman, Malachite from Russia and Diamonds from Golconda, India).

Agra Fort: It is at Yamuna ki Kinara Road, near Nehru park. The construction of this massive fort was started by Akbar and completed by his grandson Shah Jahan. This fort is in triangular shape and encircled by a massive wall two and half Kms long and 69 ft high. The fort was protected by a moat and another wall with the Yamuna river running at its base. The entrance is through Amar Singh Gate

Fatehpur Sikri : It is at 37 km south west of Agra, about 12 Kms in circumference, on a rocky ridge that over look the village of Sikri. Akbar built his capital at this village. The massive walls surround its three sides and the forth side is protected by a lake. Akbar ruled here for only 15 years. He shifted his city to Lahore and eventually back to Agra. Its styles still reflects his foresight and wisdom.

The Buland Darwaza (Victory Gateway) the main entrance was built by Akbar after he conquered Gujarat. The gate is 134 ft high and is approached by a base of steps which is another 34 ft. The Jama Masjid (Imperial Mosque) is at the right side of Buland Darwaza built around 1571 and designed to hold 10,000 worshippers. The decorations in the pillars are made in Hindu elements. The Salim Chisti (Saint) tomb is at the courtyard of Jama Masjid surrounded by walls of marble lace. The saint blessed Akbar with a much wanted male heir. Due to this the people come here and tie strings on the marble for the same blessings which he bestowed the Akbar.

Diwan-i-Am (Hall of Public Audience): It is 350 ft long, consist of cloisters surrounding a courtyard that contains the Hall of judgment. It was here that Akbar handed down the decisions, as the chief justice of his subjects, on various disputes, by sitting on his throne flanked by marble.

Jodh Bai's Palace : This palace was built for Akbar's Hindu wife, Jodh Bai. It architecture is a blend of Hindu and Muslim styles. The Hawa Mahal (The wind palace) walled by red stone screens is upstairs. The ladies of the court could peek outside unseen from here.

Corbett National Park : This oldest wild life sanctuary is just six hours from Delhi, started in 1936. It is named after the fearless hunter Jim Corbett. He lived in these hills and saved the life of many local people from the man-eater, the tiger, at the risk of his own life. The park covers 1,318 square kms.

The Ramaganga river flows through its entire length. The park can be explored by open jeep or elephant rides. There is also a watchtower in the park. The animals here include deer, monkeys and birds, wild elephants, tigers, leopards, black bear, wild boar, snakes and crocodiles. December to April is the best viewing time. Open : 16 November to 14 June, closed 15 June to 15 November.

Mussoorie : It is a hill station, 278 Km northeast of Delhi. It is in the Himalayan foothills of Uttar Pradesh at an altitude of 2000 meters. Captain Young discovered the place in 1823 and built the first British residence with club, Anglican Church (1837) and Library at Landour in 1826.

Keoladeo National Park, Bharatpur : It is 55 Km away from Agra. The people from all over the country come here to see the birds. The city was founded by the Jat ruler Suraj Mal in 1733. Now the city is famous for its popular water birds. This sanctuary is the winter home for hundreds of species of birds. The park is also home for mammals and reptiles including blue bulls, spotted deer, otter and Indian rock pythons. November to February is the best season to visit and early morning or late in the evening is the best time to see the birds.

LUCKNOW

Lucknow, also known as the "Golden city of the east", the capital of Uttar Pradesh situated along the banks of the River Gomti rose to prominence as the centre of the Nawabs of Avadh. Legend says that Lucknow derived its name from Lucknau named after Lakshmana (a character in the famous Epic Ramayana) when his elder brother Rama gave away this part of the country to him. Though it is rapidly modernising, it still has kept its past glory and is known for its cultural refinement. The huge mausoleums of the nawabs and the ruins of the Residency which stood witness to one of the most remarkable episodes in the Indian Mutiny in 1857, make it an interesting place to visit. Historically reputed as a city of culture, Lucknow is famous for its Gharana of music and chickken (shadow work embroidery) work. The best time to visit Lucknow would be winter, *i.e.*, between October and February, when the climate is pleasant and comfortable, making it easy to travel.

Bara Imambara (Tomb of a Muslim Holy Man) : The hall built by Asaf-ud-Daula for famine relief, is one of the largest in the world. There are excellent views of Lucknow from the top of the Imambara. An external stairway leads to an upper floor laid out as an amazing labyrinth known as the bhulbulaiya. The dark passages stop abruptly at openings which drop straight to the courtyard below. There's a mosque with two tall minarets in the courtyard complex and to the right of this is a well which is said to have secret tunnels opening into. The Imambara is open from morning to 6pm.

Rumi Darwaza: This huge 60-feet-high door was also built by Asaf-ud-Daula. It is also called the 'Turkish Darwaza,' it is the entrance to the Bara Imambara. It is a massive gate on the western side of the front of Bara Imambara.

Chota Imambara: Hussainabad or Chota Imambara, was built by Mohammed Ali Shah in 1837 as his own mausoleum. The appeal of this structure lies in its furnishings comprising exquisite chandeliers of Belgium glass. The glittering brass-domes and ornate architecture of this building made a Russian Prince call it the "Kremlin of India." It contains the tombs of Ali Shah and his mother. A small bazaar, known as the Gelo Khana or "Decorated Place", lies inside the imposing entrance of the Imambara.

The Clock Tower : It is located very near to the Rumi Darwaza. Built in 1881 by the British, this 67 m-high clock tower on the river Gomti is said to the tallest clock tower in India. The tower has European style artwork. The parts of the clock is built of pure gunmetal and the pendulum hangs 14 feet. The dial of this clock is shaped like a 12-petalled flower and has bells around it.

Shah Najaf Imambara: It holds the tombs of Ghasi-ud-Din Haidar and his two wife's. Situated on the south bank of Gomti towards the west of Sikandar Bagh, the building is almost an exact replica of the tomb of Hazrat Ali, the son-in-law of Prophet Muhammad, at Najaf Ashraf in Iraq. The interior is used to store chandeliers, and elaborate creations of wood, bamboo and silver paper which are carried through the streets during the Muharram Festival. It is open from 6am to 5pm.

Residency: Built in 1800 by Saadat Ali Khan for the British Resident. There is a model room in the main Residency building which is worth visiting and a small museum on the ground floor. This group of buildings became the stage for the most dramatic events of the 1857 Mutiny the Siege of Lucknow. There is cemetery near by with graves of those who suffered in the mutiny. The Residency is open from 9am to 5.30pm.

Noor Baksh: Noor Baksh Kothi (Light giving palace) is in Lal Bagh area next to the Methodist Church and now known as Noor Manzil. It was believed to be built by Saadat Ali Khan as a school for royal children while others say Agha Mir, the Prime Minister was its owner. Rafi us Shan, son of Muhammad Ali Shah made this his residence till the end of Nawabi rule. Now it houses a psychiatric clinic for the mentally disturbed.

Chattar Manzil : The two Chattar Manzils near the Begum Hazarat Mahal park, on the banks of the Gomti were Royal pavilions. The name comes from the gilt chattars or umbrellas atop the two main buildings. The Greater Chattar Manzil was once a king's palace. Under the existing river terrace was the ground floor with the tykhanas (cool underground rooms), cooled by the waters of the Gomti which lapped against its outer walls. Considering their size, surprisingly little is known about the Chattar Manzil Palaces. Today this building houses the Central Medicine Research body. The Lal Baradari was also the part of Chattar Manzil and was built as Coronation Hall and Durbar Hall.

State Museum: The state Museum in Banarasi Bagh houses an impressive collection of stone sculptures, 1st-11th century exhibits of Hindu, Buddhist and Jain works, rare coins, marble sculptures and an Egyptian Mummy. Open 10.30am to 4.30 pm except Mondays.

PARKS AND ZOO

Dudhwa National Park: Dudhwa is 238 km N of Lucknow and was designated a National Park in 1977. Bordering the Sarda River in the Terai, it is very similar to the Corbett National Park. It has sal forest, tall savannah grasslands and large marshy areas watered by the Neora and Sohel rivers. Dudhwa National Park is home to unusual animal species. This national park's star attraction is the Royal Bengal tiger. About

100 tigers are believed to still roam this region. The Indian rhino was also introduced here to save it from extinction. Leopards, elephants, bears, gharial, crocodile, and spotted deer inhabit the thick forests too.

Gautam Buddha Park - Situated in between the Bara Imambara and the Martyrs Memorial, this park has been a recreation ground for children. Rides here are a big draw. Also used by political parties to hold rallies now.

The Elephant or the Hathi Park, another recreation park.

The lemon park or the Nimbu Park of the Bara Imambara is also very popular.

Zoo : 4 km from the Charbagh station is the Lucknow Zoo or the Prince of Wales Zoological Gardens. The zoo comes under the Banarasi Bagh area. This Zoo, constructed in 1921, also has a museum, an aquarium and a toy train. The plane Rajhans used by Pandit Jawarharlal Nehru is also kept in the zoo. Open 8am to 5pm.

AYODHYA

Ram Lila: Ram Lila, the enactment of the story of Lord Rama is believed to have been started by great Saint Tulsidas. The Ramcharitmanas, written by him till today forms the basis of Ram Lila performances. In some places, Rama Lila is associated with Vijayadashmi celebrations in late September and early October and also with Rama Navami, the birthday of Lord Rama.

Ram lila, basically an enactment of a myth, is presented as a cycle-play with the story varying from 7 to 31 days. The Rama Lila performance evokes a festive atmosphere and enables observance of religious rites. It is also rich in performance of crafts such as costume jewellery, masks, headgear, make-up and decoration. The four main Ram Lila styles are the pantomimic style with a predominance of jhankis - tableaux pageants; the dialogue - based style with multi-local staging; the operative style which draws its musical elements from the folk operas of the region and the stage - Ram Lila of the professional troupes called `mandalis'.

Ayodhya is popular for mandali Ram Lila. The performance is dialogue—based and presented on a platform stage. High standard of performance is complemented by songs and kathak dances and eye-catching decor.

Ram Navmi Mela: Ayodhya, the holy city of the sacred pilgrim centre of Hindus plays host to the Ram Navmi Festival in the month of April. Thousands of worshippers gather to venerate the Lord at Kanak Bhawan.

Sravan Jhula Mela: This mela celebrates the playful spirit of the deities. On the third day of the second half of Shravan, images of the deities (specially of Rama, Lakshman and Sita) are placed in swings in the temples. They are also taken to Mani Parvat, where the idols are made to swing from the branches of the trees. Later the deities are brought back to temples. The mela lasts till the end of the month of Shravan.

Parikramas: Ayodhya is perhaps the most noted place in the northern India where parikramas are undertaken by Hindu Pilgrims. These are circumambulations of important religious places and are of varying duration, shortest being the `Antargrahi Parikrama' which has to be completed within a day. After taking a dip in the Saryu, the devotee commences the parikarma from the Nageshwarnath temple and passes through Rama Ghat, Sita Kund, Manipuravata and Brahma Kund, finally terminating at Kanak Bhawan.

Then there is the `Panchkoshi Parikrama' circuit of 10 miles, which touches Chakratirtha, Nayaghat, Ramghat, Saryubagh, Holkar-ka-pura, Dashrathkund, Jogiana, Ranopali, Jalpa Nala and Mahtabagh. On the way the people pay homage to deities in the shrines which are situated on the route.

The `Chaturdashkoshi Parikrama' constitutes a circular journey of 28 miles made once a year on the occasion of Akshainaumi, which is completed within 24 hours.

BRAJ BHOOMI

The little town comes alive with colourful festivals throughout the year. The Rang Gulal Mahotsav, held annually, celebrates Holi in an exuberant fashion. During the festival of colour which heralds the onset of spring. Several classical and folk artistes render enthralling performances.

Janmashtami, the birthday of Shri Krishna is celebrated with great pomp and splendour throughout Braj. The Raaslila is enacted recreating the many legends of Shri Krishna's life - his exploits and his amorous dalliances with the gopies. Ceremonies in the temples at midnight include the bathing of the image of infant Krishna which is then placed in a silver cradle. Songs of devotion are sung and toys offered for the amusement of the divine child. Thousands gather to offer their prayers and Mathura is astir with their devotion and celebrations.

Braj Parikrama : The Rainy month of Bhadon, the month when the Lord Krishna was born, is a time of colourful celebrations. The famous Braj Parikrama - a pilgrimage of all the places in Braj that associated with Shri Krishna, is undertaken. Traditionally, the Chaurasi kos (84 KOs) pilgrimage of Braj Mandal, with its 12 vanas (forests). 24 upvanas (groves), sacred hill Govardhan, divine River Yamuna and numerous holy places along its banks, is undertaken annually by lakhs of devotees from all over the country.

The Yatra extends to Kotban to the north of Mathura, to Nandgaon, Barsana and the Govardhan Hill to the west and Southwest of the city and to the a banks of the Yamuna to the east, where the Baldeo Temple is located. Colourful melas and performances of the Raaslila (a depiction of the exploits of Shri Krishna) are distinctive to this festive period.

Gokul: The most celebrated of Shri Krishna's abode, Gokul lies to the west of Sadabad, 1.6 km from Mahavan and 15 km southeast of Mathura, on the Mathura - Etah metalled road. It was here that Lord Krishna was brought up in secrecy by Yashoda, in the pastoral beauty of this village on the banks of the Yamuna.

Gokul attained importance during the time of Vallabhacharya (1479-1531) when it became a major centre of the Bhakti cult. The three oldest temples in the place are those dedicated to Gokulnath, Madan Mohan and Vitthalnath, said to have been built around 1511. The other temples include those of Dwarika Nath and Balkrishna in the shrines which were built in the honour of Lord Mahadeo in 1602 by Raja Vijai Singh of Jodhpur. The celebration of Janmashtami in August is unparalleled for its gaiety and melas are the constant attraction here. Other festivities celebrated with traditional fervour include the' in Bhadon, the Annakut festival and Trinavat Mela held on the fourth day of the dark half of Kartik month.

Important sites worth visiting in Gokul include the Gokulnath Temple, Raja Thakur Temple, Gopal Lalji Temple and the Morwala Temple.

VARANASI

Varanasi is commonly called as Banaras. The devout Hindus call it Kashi (resplendent with light). It has been the religious capital of Hinduism. Each Hindu devotee wants to visit Varanasi to purify their body and soul by dipping into the sacred Ganga river. This city is a temple city dedicated to Shiva.

Varanasi : Varanasi is commonly called as Banaras. The devout Hindus call it Kashi (resplendent with light). It has been the religious capital of Hinduism. Each Hindu devotee wants to visit Varanasi to purify their body and soul by dipping into the sacred Ganga river. This city is a temple city dedicated to Shiva.

Ghats : The city's life revolves around its seven km long sweep of about 100 bathing ghats that skirt the west bank of the Ganges. Most of them are used for bathing. Some are used for cremating bodies. The most sacred ghats are the Asi, Dasashwamedh Ghat, Manikarnika and Panchganga. Pilgrims who bathe in each one consecutively believe their prayers will be fulfilled. A short boat trip from Manikarnika Ghat can be an interesting introduction to the river.

It is believed that cremation at Manikarnika ghat ensures a safe place in Heaven, as the cremators of this ghat are believed to have the patronage of Shiva. The furthermost upstream ghat is Assi Ghat, which marks the confluence of the Ganges and the Assi rivers. It is said that after striking down demon Shumbha and nishumbha, Durga's sword fell and created a curved ditch, which later became the Assi Channel.

This Ghat is one of the five special ghats which pilgrims are supposed to bathe at in sequence during the ritual route called ' Panchatirthi Yatra' ending in the Adikeshva ghat in the north. Nearby is the Tulsi Ghat, where Goswami Tulsidas lived till his death in 1623 AD. The Bachra Ghat is used by Jains and there are three riverbank Jain Temples. The Dandi Ghat is used by fakirs, yogis and ascetics and nearby is the very popular Hanuman Ghat. Dashashvamedh Ghat, Varanasi's liveliest bathing place was constructed by Peshwa Balaji Baji Rao.

It's name indicates that Brahma sacrificed (medh) 10 (das) horses (aswa) here. It's one of the most important ghats and is conveniently central. Nearby is the grand Man Mandir Ghat (1637) and an observatory both built by Sawai Raja Jai Singh of Jaipur in 1710. Mir Ghat leads to a Nepalese temple, which has erotic sculptures. Dattatreya Ghat bears the footprint of the Brahmin saint of that name in a small temple nearby.

The Ram Ghat was built by the Raja of Jaipur. Panchaganga Ghat, where India's five holy rivers are said to merge. The Trilochan Ghat has two turrets emerging from the river, and the water between them is especially holy. Another important cremation ghat is the Hirishchandra ghat, named after the king Harishchandra who worked as a cremator at the cremation grounds.

The best time to visit the ghats is at dawn when the river is bathed in a magical light and pilgrims come to perform puja to the rising sun. The best view of the Ghats can be had from a boat midstream or from the Malviya bridge. Burning pyres, people getting their hair shaved off, the chanting of sacred slokas, giving of alms to Brahmins, Pandas (Brahmin Priests) sitting under huge umbrellas offering prayers for their clients, devotees praying and drinking water from the holy river are the common sight at these ghats.

Sarnath: The Buddha came to this hamlet, 10 Km. north-east of Varanasi, to preached his message "Maha-Dharma-Chakra Pravartan" (in Buddhist terminology, 'turned the wheel of the law') after he achieved enlightment at Bodhigaya. Later, the great Buddhist Emperor Ashoka built here the Dharmarajika Stupa and near it erected a pillar surmounted by the magnificent capital of four adored lions, which today forms the national emblem of India. Ashoka erected several memorial towers or stupas.

Saranath probably derived its name from one of Buddha's title, Saranganath, Lord of the Deer. The Chinese Buddhist pilgrims, Fa-hsien and Hiuen Tsiang who visited in the 5th and 7th centuries respectively, both recorded impressions of their stay.

The huge swastika (110ft) covered Dhameskh Stupa dates from AD 500 and is thought to mark the place where Buddha gave his sermon. Sarnath has been a premier centre for Buddhism. It is a rich collection of ancient Buddhist relics and antiques comprising numerous Buddha and Bodhisatva images on display at the excellent Archaeological Museum (open 10am to 5pm except on Friday).

Saranath's annual festival is Buddha Purnima, which commemorates Buddha's birth with colourful fair and procession of his relics held on the full moon of May/June. Ramnagar

The residential place of Kashi Naresh (Former Maharaja of Varanasi) across the Ganges at Ramnagar houses a museum with the exhibits of palanquins, costumes, swords, sabres, etc. Dussehra celebration of Ramnagar is an interesting event to witness 14 km. from Varanasi.

The fort at Ramnagar houses a museum displaying the Royal collection which includes vintage cars, Royal palkies, an armoury of swords and old guns, ivory work and antique clock. The Durga Temple and Chhinnamastika Temple are also located at Ramnagar.

FORT AND PALACE

Chunar Fort: The Chunar fort is situated 40 Km. from Varanasi. Chunar Fort, overlooking the Ganges, has had a succession of owners representing most of India's rulers over the last 500 years. Sher Shah took it from Humayun in 1540, Akbar recaptured it for the Mughals in 1575 and in the 18th century it passed to the nawabs of Avadh. They were shorty followed by the British, whose gravestones here make interesting reading. Chunar sandstone has been used for centuries, most famously in Ashokan pillars - and is still quarried, leaving the surrounding hills looking ravaged in places.

Ram Nagar Fort and Palace : Ramnagar Fort which was built in 1750 AD by the Maharaja of Banaras, is on the right bank of River Ganga. Built of red stones, it provides strength and stability to the city. Visit : Daily from 0900 to 1200 and 1400 - 1500. It is the residential palace of the former Maharaja of Varanasi. The palace is an astronomical and astrological wonder. Inside the giant walls of the palace, there is a big clock. Besides showing year, month, week and day, it baffles the onlooker with astronomy of the sun, moon and constellation of stars.

This wonder clock or Dharam Ghari was made by the court astronomer of Banaras in 1852 AD. The palace has a temple dedicated to Ved Vyas and a museum set up by the last Maharaja of Banaras, Vibhuti Narain Singh. The museum has a collection of brocade costumes, palanquins, weapons and has expensive coaches made of ivory. The palace is decorated majestically and it vibrates with colour and life, during Dussehra festival. The celebrations comes to an end on Vijayadashmi, when the huge effigies of demon king Ravana and his kinsmen are sent up in flames, signifying the victory of good over evil.

ABC Art Gallery : This gallery is situated opposite of Tulsi Manas Mandir, Durga Kund Road. Opens from 1500 to 1900. Entry - free. This gallery exhibits the work of well known artists of India. It gives a picture of the contemporary culture of Varanasi.

B.H.U. & Bharat Kala Bhavan Museum: Banaras Hindu University (B.H.U) founded by Pandit Madan Mohan Malviya in 1917 AD is the largest residential University in India. At the entrance, there is the grand statue of its founder and the Vishwanath temple in its centre. The huge temple was built in 1966, under patronage of the Birlas. It has a 677 meter high rising white top and its well carved architecture attracts pilgrims.

In the cool and calm surroundings of B.H.U is the Bharat Kala Bhavan which has established in 1920 AD and has a vast collection of paintings, Hindu and Buddhist sculptures and other materials of archeological studies. In the main hall of the Bhawan, there is a figure of a man standing on one leg and one hand on his hip and lifting a mass of stone above his head, with one hand. The figure is said to be of Lord Krishna lifting Govardana. In the halls of the Bharat Kala Bhawan, there are many rare images that testify to the existence of Krishna cult in Kashi in 15th and 16th century Gupta period. It has the miniature paintings from the courts of Mughals and the Hindu Princes of Punjab Hills. Visit : Monday to Saturday. Opens from 1030 to 1600.

Ashoka Pillar : It is at Saranath, 10km north of Varanasi. Sarnath, the place where Buddha gave his first sermon is a popular Buddhist pilgrimage centre. The Ashoka pillar stands in front of the main stupa where Ashoka sat and meditated. The Sarnath Archaeological Museum at Ashoka Marg, houses a copy of Ashoka's lion pillar and some sculptures. Click for more details on Sarnath (Deer park).

TEMPLES AND MOSQUES

Vishwanath Temple (Golden Temple): The most sacred temple in Varanasi is the Vishwanath temple, located at Vishvanath Gali dedicated to Lord Shiva. Hindus believe Shiva lives here, so it's far too holy a place for non-Hindus to view, the followers of other religions are permitted a view from the Naubat Khana (seat of temple choir). The shivalinga at the Vishwanath temple is among one of the 12 Jyotrilingas.

The current temple was built in 1776 by Ahalya Bai of Indore with about 800 kg of gold plating on the towers, which gives the temple its colloquial name, Golden Temple. The gold plated spire, was the gift of the Sikh Maharaja Ranjit Singh of Lahore in 1835, more than 50 years later. The well of wisdom or 'Gyan Vapi' which is nearby is believed to have been built by Lord Shiva himself to cool the 'linga' of Vishwanath with water.

Durga Temple: It was built in the 18th century by a Bengali maharani and is stained red with ochre. The Durga Temple is commonly known as the Monkey Temple due to the many frisky monkeys that have made in their home. Non-Hindus can enter the courtyard but not the inner sanctum.

Kedareshvara Temple : It is the most important Shiva temple of the city. The stone linga here is said to have emerged spontaneously. The myth narrate that a pure hearted devotee of Shiva prayed for a chance to visit the famous Kedareshvara Shiva temple in the Himalayas. Shiva, who is the god of destruction is always kind to his bhaktas (devotees). Shiva was touched by his bhakta's piety and instead of bringing him to the mountain, Shiva brought his image to the bhakta. This image (linga) emerged out of a plate of rice and lentils. It can be still seen by the believers on the rough surface of the natural stone linga.

Sankat Mochan Temple : It is at Durga Kund Road. The word Sankat Mochan means deliverer from troubles. The temple belongs to Hanuman (monkey God), an incarnation of Vishnu. The best time to visit this temple is in the early evening.

Shitala Temple : This white temple is dedicated to Shitala, the smallpox goddess. It is situated at Shitala Ghat. The Santoshi Mata (Mother of Contentment) shrine is added to this temple.

Chausath Yogini Temple : This temple is situated just above the Chausath Yogini Ghat. It was originally devoted to a tantric cult. Now it is devoted to Kali. The deity here is known as 'Ma' (mother).

Gyanvapi Mosque : This mosque was built by Mughal emperor Aurangazeb. The foundation and the rear part of the mosque are the remains of a temple. One of its minarets which dominated the skyline of the holy city, collapsed in the 1948 floods.

Alamgir Mosque : This mosque was constructed by Aurangazeb. It is a blend of Hindu and Muslim designs. A famous bathing point, Panjaganga Ghat lies below it.

ALLAHABAD

Allahabad built on a very ancient site of the Aryans formerly known as Prayag, is located at the junction of the holy rivers Ganga and the Yamuna. The city acquired its present name in 1584 under the Mughal Emperor Akbar, who named it Al-Ilahabad (the city of God). The 'Maha Kumbh Mela' believed to be one of the largest religious gathering in the world, is held every 12 years at the confluence of the holy rivers attracting millions of Hindu devotees. This historically famous city was a centre of the Indian Independence movement and the home of the Nehru family. Today Allahabad is a rapidly growing commercial and administrative city in Uttar Pradesh. The climate of Allahabad is one of the extreme types with annual range of temperature differing around 12°C. The best time to visit Allahabad is from the month of November to February.

Sangam: The sacred 'Sangam' is the confluence of three of the holiest rivers in Hindu mythology Ganga, Yamuna and the mythical underground river of enlightenment, Saraswati. At the confluence, the muddy waters of the Ganges and the clear green water of the Yamuna can be distinctly seen to merge into one.

Bathing at the Sangam is believed to be auspicious through out the year especially for 15 days in the month of Magh (mid-January to Mid-February) during 'Magh Mela' and longer during Maha Kumbh Mela held every 12 years. Astrologers calculate the holiest time to enter the water and draw up a 'Holy Dip Schedule'. Maha Kumbh Mela attracts millions of devout Hindus and a holy dip then is believed to cleanse the soul. An enormous temporary township springs up on the vacant land on the Allahabad side of the river.

Allahabad Fort: The massive majestic fort built by Emperor Akbar in 1583 A.D fort stands on the banks of the Yamuna near the confluence. The largest of Akbar's forts, it was matchless in its design and construction. Now used by the army, prior permission is needed for a visit except for a limited area open to visitors. The fort has massive walls and three gateways flanked by high towers. Inside the fort there is the Zenana (harem) and the 3rd century BC Ashoka pillar moved to the fort from Kausambi, 'Saraswati Koop'; a well, said to be the source of the Saraswati river, Patalpuri, the underground temple and the much-revered 'Akshaya Vata' or immortal Banyan tree within the temple.

The Ashoka pillar standing 10.6 meters high has several edicts and a Persian inscription of Emperor Jahangir encrypted on it, commemorating his accession to the throne.

Khusrau Bagh: Khusrau Bagh located near the railway station, contains the tomb of Prince Khusrau son of the Mughal emperor Jehangir, who was jailed and executed after an unsuccessful rebellion and a plot to assassinate his father. The typical Mughal Garden enclosure is entered through an 18m high archway. Nearby is the tomb believed to be his sisters and the two storied tomb of his Rajput mother.

Allahabad Museum: Allahabad Museum located at Kamala Nehru Road inside Chandra Shekhar Azad Park, has 18 galleries containing a wide range of stone sculptures. The sculptures include 2nd BC pieces from Bharhut and Kausambi, 1st Century AD Kushana from Mathura, 4th-6th century Gupta and 11th century carvings from Khajuraho. The exhibit also has terracotta figurines from Kausambi, Rajasthani Miniatures, coins and paintings by Nicholas Roerich and artifacts donated by the Nehru family. Open daily from 10:30 am to 4:30 PM except Mondays.

Anand Bhawan: Anand Bhavan was the former ancestral home of the Nehru family. Donated to the Indian government in 1970 by Indira Gandhi, it was turned into a museum. The exhibits in the two storied building seen through glass panels include personal items of Motilal Nehru, Jawaharlal Nehru; the first Prime Minister of Independent India, Indira Gandhi (Prime Minister 1966-77, 1980-84) and her sons Sanjay Gandhi and Rajeev Gandhi (Prime Minister 1984-1989). One can see the room where Mahatma Gandhi used to stay during his visits, Jawarlal Nehru's room and study also. Open: 9:30 am to 05:00 pm. except Mondays.

There is a Jawahar planetarium build in 1979 in the compound. Open 11:00 am to 04:00 pm. except Mondays

Swaraj Bhawan: Situated next to Anand Bhawan, Swaraj Bhavan was donated to the Nation by Moti Lal Nehru to be used as the headquarters of the Congress Committee. Late Prime Minister of India, Mrs. Indira Gandhi was born here.Open: 09:30 am to 05:30 P.M. Closed on Monday's.

Muir Central College—University of Allahabad: Designed by William Emerson and opened in 1886, the college is a fine example of 'Indo-saracenic' architecture. It has a 200 feet tower made of pale-yellow sandstone with marble and mosaic floors. It was later established as the University of Allahabad, one of the most reputed Universities of India. The University has Kausambi Museum with various artifacts from Kausambi including pottery, Terracotta figurines, coins, beads and bangles.

Minto Park or Madan Mohan Malviya Park: Minto Park is located to the west of the fort near the Yamuna river. It was here that the East India Company officially handed over control of India to the British government in 1858. Lord Canning read out the declaration. There is a stone memorial with a four-lion symbol on top here.

Chandra Shekhar Azad Park: Earlier known as Alfred park, thisextensive garden park has some fine colonial Buildings, including a public library. Later the park was renamed in honour of the freedom fighter Chandra Shekhar Azad who died in an encounter with the imperialists. Within the park is the Allahabad Museum.

PLACES AROUND ALLAHABAD

Kausambi: Kausambi earlier known as Kausam is located 63 km southwest of Allahabad on the way to Chitrakoot. This ancient Buddhist and Jain centre was the capital of the Vatsa king Udayana.

Buddha has delivered several discourses in this historical city. Kausambi was first discovered by Cunningham and the coins and terracotta figurines which scattered here are now on display in the Allahabad Museum and the Kausambi Museum. Recent discoveries are made by G R Sharma of the University of Allahabad. The remains of an Ashoka pillar, a palace in ruins are of Archeological interest here. Another Ashokan pillar was removed to Allahabad fort by the Mughals. There is also a Digambar Jain temple here.

Bhita: Situated 18km from Allahabad on the Yamuna river. Excavations here have revealed the remains of an ancient fortified city. There a Museum which exhibits stone and metal seals, coins and terracotta statues dating from Gupta and Mauryan periods.

Garhwa: Situated 50 km from Allahabad in Garhwa there is a walled enclosure surrounding a group of ruins of temples where several inscriptions dedicated to Vishnu and Shiva can be seen. To the west of the ruins of the fort, there is a big tank knwon as Garhwa Tal. Some of the sculptures of the Gupta period found here has been shifted to the State Museum in Lucknow.

Kara: Situated 69 km from Allahabad on the banks of Ganga, it is famous for the holy Temple of Kara Devi (Shitala Devi). Once the provincial capital of Mughals, its ruins extend to 3.5 km along Ganga. Kalehswar Mahadev Temple, Dargah of Khwaja Karak and Shivala Maharishi Ashram are the other attractions.

Chitrakoot: Chitrakoot 132km from Allahabad is a popular Hindu pilgrimage centre. Bathing ghats line the Mandakini river and there are over 30 temples in this town. Brahma,

Vishnu and Shiva are believed to have taken their incarnations and Lord Ram has stayed here during his exile. There are many places of religious interest here- Kamadgiri, Ramghat, Janki Kund, Hanuman Dhara, Gupt Godavari, Sati Ansuiya Ashram are some of them.

Kanpur: Kanpur, situated on the banks of the holy river Ganga, stands as one of North India's major industrial centers with its own historical, religious and commercial importance. It is believed to be founded by king Hindu Singh of the erstwhile state of Sachendi. During the war of 1857, it was the headquarters of a large Indian garrison and was called 'Cawnpore'. It still bears landmarks of the British Raj. Today, it is essentially a commercial and industrial centre. Besides its leather industry a large number of textile, plastic and other factories are located here. For this reason, Kanpur is also known as, `the Manchester of the East'. Best time to visit Kanpur is October to March.

The Kanpur Memorial Church (All Soul's Cathedral): The Kanpur Memorial Church built in 1875, was designed by Walter Granville. This Gothic style building has fine stained glass windows and interesting memorials. There is a Memorial Garden on the eastern side. There is a carved gothic screen, designed by Henry Yule and in the centre there is a beautifully carved figure of an angel by Baron Carlo Marochetti, representing the 'symbol of peace'. The Cemetery has a number of graves from the late 19th century.

Jain Glass Temple: It is situated in Maheshwari Mohal behind the Kamla Tower. It is a beautiful temple highly decorated with glass and enamel works.

Jajmau: Jajmau, known as Siddhapuri in ancient times, is supposed to have been the kingdom of Yayati, the Pauranic king and the high mound overhanging the Ganga is known as the site of his fort. Excavations of the Jajmau mound during 1957-58 unearthed antiquities ranging from 600 BC to 1600 AD. Now, Jajmau houses the Siddhnath and Siddha Devi temples and the mausoleum of Makhdum Shah Ala-ul-Haq, the famous Sufi saint, built by Firoz Shah Tughlaq in 1358. A mosque built by Kulich Khan in 1679 is also here.

Shri Radhakrishna Temple : This beautifully constructed temple is a unique blend of ancient and modern architecture. The even-level roofs of the mandaps have been provided with adequate ventilation for sufficient light and air. Among the five shrines in the temple, the central one is dedicated to Shri Radhakrishna and the others have idols of Shri Laxminarayan, Shri Ardhanarishwar, Shri Narmadeshwar and Shri Hanuman. This temple was built by J.K. Trust.

Phool Bagh (Ganesh Udyan): It is a beautiful park in the heart of the city on the Mall Road. In the centre of the park there is a Ganesh Shanker Vidyarthi Memorial generally used for public meetings. The annual flower shows are held here. It has a Summer House and a large Public library.

Kamla Retreat: Situated on Kamala Nehru road, Kamla Retreat houses a museum which has a good collection of historical and archaeological artifacts. Besides parks and a canal with facilities for boating, a zoo is also here. Visitors are allowed only with prior permission from:; Deputy General Manager (Administration), Kamla Tower, Kamalanagar, Kanpur, UP.

PARKS AND ZOO

Nana Rao Park: Formerly known as Memorial Well Garden, it is the biggest park in Kanpur and is situated in the heart of the city on the Mall Road. After Independence, it has been renamed after Nana Rao Peshwa, the hero of the first War of independence in 1857. It is very beautifully laid out and has a plant nursery.

Brijendra Swarup Park : Situated in Aryanagar area of Kanpur, this park has spacious lawns and play grounds.

Moti Jheel : This is drinking water reservoir of Kanpur Waterworks. It is situated Benajhabar area of the city. The area around the Jheel or lake have lately been developed into a beautiful recreation grounds and children's park.

Green Park: This is the best and most famous play ground of Kanpur. International Cricket matches are held here and it is one of the best pitches in the world.

Allen Forest Zoo: The Kanpur Zoo was opened in 1971 and ranks among one of the best zoos in the country. It is an ideal place for picnics in picturesque surroundings.

8

Population and Religion

POPULATION

The total population of the state was 8.8 crores in 1971. It increased to 11.1 crores in 1981 and then reported to be 13.9 crores in 1991. The increase, in population in these two decades was almost identical at 25 per cent. As against this, the national population shows a declining trend from 25 per cent in 1971-81 to 23.8 per cent in 1981-91. Since 1971-81 the decadal variation of U.P. population in percentage forms has remained higher than that of the national.

With over 175 million inhabitants, Uttar Pradesh is the most populous state in India and is also the most populous country subdivision in the world. Only five countries (the People's Republic of China, India itself, the United States, Indonesia and Brazil) have a higher population (see List of countries by population).

According to Indian Census 2001, 81% of the population follows Hinduism while second largest religious group is Muslim at about 18%. The people are of Indo-Aryan stock

Despite carving out a separate State of Uttaranchal from Uttar Pradesh, the State still way ahead of all States and Union territories in terms of population. Its population as at 0:00 hours of 1st March 2001 stood at 166,052,859 as per the provisional results of the Census of India 2001.

The population of the State rose by 25.80% during the decade 1991-2001. The sex ratio (*i.e.*, the number of females per thousand males) of population is recorded as 898, which has improved from 876 worked out during the previous census. Total literacy of the State rose to 57.36% from 40.71% in 1991.

Population

Persons	:	166,052,859
Males	:	87,466,301
Females	:	78,586,558
Sex Ratio	:	898

Population (0-6 years)

Persons	:	30,472,042
Males	:	15,903,900
Females	:	14,568,142
Sex Ratio (0-6 years)	:	916

Number of Literates

Persons	:	77,770,275
Males	:	50,256,119
Females	:	27,514,156

Decadal Growth 1991-2001

Persons	:	(+) 25.80 %
Males	:	(+) 24.31 %
Females	:	(+) 27.50 %

Percentage of Population (0-6) to Total Population

Persons	:	18.35 %
Males	:	18.18 %
Females	:	18.54 %

Percentage of Literates to Total Population

Persons	:	57.36 %
Males	:	70.23 %
Females	:	42.98 %

DEMOGRAPHICS

Religions in Uttar Pradesh (2011)

Hinduism (79.73%)

Islam (19.26%)

Sikhism (0.32%)

Christianity (0.18%)

Jainism (0.11%)

Buddhism (0.10%)

Other religions and Not stated (0.30%)

Uttar Pradesh has a large population and a high population growth rate. From 1991 to 2001 its population increased by over 26%. Uttar Pradesh is the most populous state in India, with 199,581,477 people on 1 March 2011. The state contributes 16.16% of India's population. The population density is 828 people per square kilometre, making it one of the most densely populated states in the country.

The sex ratio in 2011, at 912 women to 1000 men, was lower than the national figure of 943. The state's 2001–2011 decennial growth rate (including Uttrakhand) was 20.09%, higher than the national rate of 17.64%. Uttar Pradesh has a large number of people living below the poverty line. Estimates released by the Planning Commission for the year 2009–10 revealed that Uttar Pradesh had 59 million people below the poverty line, the most for any state in India.

As per 2011 census, Uttar Pradesh, the most populous state in India, is home to the highest numbers of both Hindus and Muslims. By religion, the population in 2011 was Hindus 79.73%, Muslims 19.26%, Sikhs 0.32%, Christians 0.18%, Jains 0.11%, Buddhists 0.10%, and Others 0.30%. The literacy rate of the state at the 2011 census was 67.7%, which was below the national average of 74%. The literacy rate for men is 79% and for women 59%. In 2001 the literacy rate in Uttar Pradesh stood at 56.27% overall, 67% for men and 43% for women.

Hindi is the official language of Uttar Pradesh and is spoken by the majority of the population (91.32%), although different regions have their own dialects. These include Awadhi spoken in the Awadh region of eastern Uttar Pradesh, Bhojpuri spoken in the Bhojpuri region of eastern Uttar Pradesh, and Braj Bhasha spoken in the Braj region western Uttar Pradesh. Urdu is given the status of a second official language.

Demographics of Uttar Pradesh

The demographics of Uttar Pradesh is a complex topic, which is undergoing dynamic change. Uttar Pradesh is India's most populous state. It has a population of about 227,920,005 as per the 2011 census. If it were a separate country, Uttar Pradesh would be the world's fifth most populous nation, next only to China, India, the United States of America and Indonesia. Uttar Pradesh has a population more than that of Pakistan. There is an average population density of 828 persons per km^2 i.e. 2,146 per sq mi. The capital of Uttar Pradesh is Lucknow. Hindus and Muslims consider the state as a holy place.

The peripheral regions of Uttar Pradesh, are home to a number of tribal communities such as Agaria, Baiga, Bhar, Bhoksa, Bind, Chero, Gond, Kol and Korwa. Five of these tribal communities have been recoginised by the Government of India as disadvantaged scheduled tribes, viz. Tharus, Boksas, Bhotias, Jaunswaris and Rajis. The Literacy rate of the state according to the 2011 Census is 70.69%. With the literacy rate for Males at 79.20%, while it is 59.30% for the Females. While this is still below the national average of 74.04% (82.14% for men, 65.16% for women) the rate of growth has been much higher in Uttar Pradesh as compared to the rest of India

Racial and ancestral makeup

Uttar Pradesh is the most populous state in India with a population of over 199.5 million people on 1 March 2011. It is more populated than the world's 242 countries. If independent it would be the 6th largest country in the world as per Population. At the 2001 census of India, about 80% of Uttar Pradesh population is Hindu, while Muslims make up around 18% of the population. The remaining population consists of Sikhs,

Buddhists, Christians and Jains. The population of Uttar Pradesh is divided into numerous castes and sub-castes. Historically, Hindu society is divided into four sub-divisions or varnas, the Brahmins, Kshatriyas, Vaishyas and Shudras. Muslims are also divided as the Shias and Sunnis. In actual practice, Hindu society in generally used to be divided into numerous lineage groups called jatis. Each jati is then sub-divided into clans, called gotras.

The peripheral regions of Uttar Pradesh, are home to a number of tribal communities such as Agaria, Baiga, Bhar, Bhoksa, Chero, Gond, Kol and Korwa. Five of these tribal communities have been recoginised by the Government of India as disadvantaged scheduled tribes, viz. Tharus, Boksas, Bhotias, Jaunswaris and Rajis.

PEOPLE

Uttar Pradesh is the most populous state in the Indian Union. Kanpur is the biggest city in the state. Other big cities are Agra, Varanasi and Allahabad.

The Brahmins, Kshatriyas and Vaishyas, the three upper castes people of the state who have dominated the political and economic scene over the centuries are in a minority. A major group comprises of the backward classes, scheduled castes and tribes. The tribal population is largely concentrated in the hill, terai-bhabhar and Vindhya regions. The central government has recognised five of the tribal communities, *viz.* Tharus, Bhoksas, Bhotias, Jaunswaris and Rajis as scheduled tribes. Besides the upper class, there are also other Hindu and Muslim communities. The scheduled castes and scheduled tribes live in rural areas and are mostly dependent on agriculture, forming the landless labour class.

HINDUS

The central fact of the social order in Uttar Pradesh is the existence of the caste system among the Hindus who constitute the vast majority of the population. The state has a number of citadels of Hindu orthodoxy which from very ancient times laid down the law for the Hindus and have had a profound influence on their life and behaviour. Great movements of reform have also originated from these citadels, which influenced and changed the social structure of the society.

The broad hierarchy in the Hindu social system were the Brahmins, Kshatriyas, Vaishyas, Shudras and achhuts or untouchables. Further division based on occupation gave rise to castes like nai (barber), dhobi (washer man), lohar (blacksmith), darzi (tailor) and all of them formed a vital part of the village economy and life.

Under economic pressure some Brahmins in Eastern Uttar Pradesh, way back in an undetermined past, took to tilling the land themselves. This was a taboo for Brahmins in this area and they became outcastes. A separate sub-caste, which is lower than the full blooded Brahmins in hierarchy but higher than the Kshatriyas, thereby came into existence, known as Bhumihars. Several other of Khatris and Bishnois can be cited. These arose out of an intermixture of blood and other factors.

The rigid caste attitude in the past and the social and political tensions have resulted in the growth of large settlements of particular castes in compact regions in Uttar Pradesh. Thus there are a large pockets of Ahirs, Gujars, Kurmis, Bhumihars and so on in different parts. The scheduled castes and the Harijans have their own settlement everywhere. The village leadership is in the hands of the upper castes while in the Urban areas, the trading class (Vaishyas), with plenty of money to spend, is a well-knit community and has a large say in the direction of affairs.

MUSLIMS

The Muslims are not evenly distributed over the state. They are found in western divisions of Meerut, Agra and Rohilkhand and in the eastern districts in the terai area, in Gonda and Bahraich, in Azamgarh, Jaunpur and Ghazipur.

The fertile plains of Uttar Pradesh offered an ideal habitat for the early Muslim settlers who came in the wake of the establishment of Turkish rule in India. The hostility was confined mainly within the ruling classes - The Rajas, Rawats, Rais and the original village echelons and the muqtis and their subordinates. Years before the Ghurid conquest of northern India, the Muslims had settled in Badaun, Bahraich, Kannauj, Unnao and Bilgram.

Muslim concentration in towns was primarily due to their socio-political organizations, their exclusive racial and religious complexion. Muslims have always had an influential upper class consisting of Nawabs, Rajas and Chaudhries because of their historical antecedents. Included in this class, before zamindari abolition, was a large retinue of personal staff and hangers-on (musahibs) who maintained the airs of their aristocratic masters and liked to be classified along with them.

The middle class, comparatively thin among Muslims, is engaged in the traditional trades like leather, timber (in the terai area), tobacco and perfume (in Lucknow). There is only a sprinkling of Muslims in the services and professions. Commerce and trade was not a Muslim forte.

Muslims have overwhelmingly large lower class, appallingly poor, conservative and hide-bound. It consists of artisans, petty traders, weavers, carpet makers, labourers, butchers, hide-flayers, vegetable-settlers and the like. They have no independent thinking and are guided solely by their religious leaders. The Muslims are stratified into four broad divisions. There were Sayyid, Shaikh, Mughal and Pathan.

These four broad divisions and their further sub-divisions are besides the two principal sects in which Muslims can be classified - Sunnis and Shias. The Shias form a fractional minority and are concentrated mostly in Lucknow, Jaunpur and Amroha. Their number is less than that of Sunnis. The former Nawabs of Avadh and Rampur were Shias. Only in Lucknow the Shias form an influential minority among Muslims.

The caste system among Muslims has outgrown its rigidity. Intermarriages among Shias and Sunnis take place, not to speak of intermarriages among Sunni castes themselves and there are no inter-dining or pollution taboos. A process of raising of caste status is prevalent among the Muslim. The term

'Ashrafization' has been coined for the process of elevation of lower ranks on the Ashraf pattern. The purdah or seclusion of women had become a common practice. With the abolition of Zamindari, the upper class—the landed aristocracy - has vanished into thin air.

TRIBES

Note: A part of Uttar Pradesh mainly tribal areas with the following districts such as Dehradun, Uttarkashi, Tehri Garhwal, Rudraprayag, Chamoli, Hardwar, Pauri Garhwal, Bageswar, Pithoragarh, Almora, Nainital, Champawat and Udham Singh Nagar has been formed into a new state Uttaranchal. So part of the tribal population is now in the state of Uttaranchal.

The population of the tribal communities in the state is not large. They constitute the weakest section of the society and form distinct ethnic groups which have preserved their own separate culture identities in their original environment despite the ravages of time.

The tribes live in three well-defined regions - the mountain tracts of Garhwal, Kumaon and Uttrakhand, the terai-bhabhar area extending from Dehra Dun to Bahraich district and the Vindhyan tracts of Mizapur, Allahabad, Varanasi and Bundelkhand. They also live in Pithoragarh, Uttarkashi, Tehri, Banda and Jhansi districts.

Garhwal, Kumaon, Pithoragarh, Uttarkashi and Chamoli have the habitats of the Bora, Bhotia and Raji tribes. The Jaunsari type of tribal groups include the Khasas of the Jamuna tract of Dehra Dun district who claim to be Rajputs and Brahmins and the Aujis, Doms and Kolis, Koisor Koltas who are Harijans. The Jaunsari types are also found in the adjoining areas of Rawain (Uttarkashi) and Jaunpur (Tehri). The Bhoksas and the Tharus inhabit the Terai-bhabhar area. The Vindhyan tracts have the largest number of tribes, including Agaria, Bhil, Bhumiyar, Chero, Ghasia, Gond, Kol, Korwaa, Oroan, Parahiya, Panika, Pathari and Sahariya. The Jaunsaris are numerically the largest group.

Only five of the states tribal communities have been recognised by the central government as scheduled tribes in terms of the provisions of the constitution. They are the Bhotia, Bhoksa, Jaunsari, Raji and Tharu tribes, inhabiting the sensitive border area. The remaining tribes with the exception of Bhil, Bora and sections of the polyandrous people of Uttarkashi and Tehri, are termed as scheduled castes.

Tharus and Bhoksas are of Mongoloid stock and the Khasas of the Himalayan region of Indo-Aryan stock. The remaining Jaunsari types are of mixed descent. Of the Vindhyan tribes, the Gonds and Kols belong to Munda-Dravidian stock. The Bhils and Saharujas are of Indo-Dravidian origin.

The tribal areas suffered from poor communications and roads were unsuitable for the major portion of the year. There was extreme scarcity of water during summer, specially in Mirzapur and Banda districts. The Bhotias of the northern frontier suffered a severe setback on account of sudden stoppage of trade with Tibet.

The Jaunsaris, had little land of their own and generally worked as labourers on farms or in forests. The problems of Tharus and Bhoksas in the terai areas were quite different. Those lands which were previously defined as fallow land, were captured and developed by this community. The development had already been completed, thousands of outsiders and fortune-seekers were trying to come over and prosper at the cost of local tribes by displacing them from their paternal land. The state governments efforts to meet the situation had met with only partial success.

The Khasas are at the top in the Jaunsar tract and the Gonds in the Mirzapur region. For the Khasas, the Koltas do the tilling of land while the Bajgis are their tailors and the Lohars and Sonars their blacksmiths and goldsmiths. The Agarias, Panikas and Ghasias do services for the Gonds, though the Gonds have now lost their hegemony. All the tribes love liquor. The Dangwarias and Kathawaras among the Tharus make their own brand of rice beer. The Korwas and Rajis live on wild fruit and tree roots. The tribals now wear the same kind of dress as non-tribals but the tribal women's weakness for gaudy dress, ornaments and finery is pronounced.

The tribes have their own separate pantheons but they also worship a few Hindu gods. The Kols of Banda are devotees of Rama, Sita and Lakshmana because of their legendary association with them during their sojourn in exile at Chitrakut. The Sahariyas claim their descent from Shabari, the poor Bhil woman whose hospitality Lord Rama accepted during his wandering in the Chitrakut forests.

The tribals follow the patriarchal and patrilineal order of society. Women have a high social status. Among the Tharus of Naini Tal they play a more dominant role than men. Polygamy is a status symbol. Polyandry is prevalent among the Jaunsaris. The Korwas and Bhotias have a custom by which on the death of the elder brother the younger brother can claim the widow. Song and dance are part of the tribal way of life. Among the Jaunsaris and Bhotias, both men and women dance. The Kols have only women dancers. For Bhoksa women dancing is taboo, while Tharu women dance during Holi only. Bhoksas, Tharus and Sahariyas have organized male-dancing parties.

9

Art, Architecture, Fair and Festivals

ART AND CRAFT

Uttar Pradesh is famous for its rich heritage of art and craft. Most famous centres are the following:

- Agra since the Mughal era has been home to numerous Mughal crafts, including the *Pietra Dura*, still practised today.
- Aligarh is famous for its Lock around the world; Aligarh boasts for its Zari work, (a type of fabric decoration), 'Jhumka' – an intricate ear-rings or ear-pendants, Manja and Surma (Kohl (cosmetics)), despite all these craft work, painter S. A. Jafar represent Aligarh in the field of fine arts across the India and abroad.
- Firozabad, the city of bangles, is also a hub for crafting many glass accessories. The glass artefacts produced in its factories are of high value and are exported all over the country and around the world.
- Kannauj is well known for oriental perfumes, scents and rose water and also for traditional tobacco products.
- Khurja is famous for its ceramics pottery; in fact, the entire state is famous for its pottery not only in India but also around the world.

- Lucknow, the capital, boasts of its cloth work and embroidery (chikan) work on silk and cotton garments.
- Allahabad(Prayagraj) is known for its National Institute of Art & Craft College.
- Bhadohi is known for its carpets, a craft which dates back to the 16th century, during the reign of Mughal Emperor, Akbar and is believed to have established when centuries ago, some Iranian master weavers stopped at Madhosingh village, near Khamaria, in Bhadohi while travelling in India, and subsequently set up looms here. Bhadohi carpets received the Geographical Indication (GI) tag in 2010, and also known as dollar-city; beside this, it is one of the highest revenue generating districts of UP.
- Moradabad is well known for its metal-ware, especially brass artefacts.
- Pilibhit is known for its wooden footwear (locally called Paduka or Khadaon) and also for flutes made of wooden pipes. Flutes are exported to Europe, America and other countries.
- Saharanpur is known all over India and abroad for its wood-carving items produced there.
- Varanasi Mubarakpur, Azamgarh is famous for its Banarasi saris and silk. A *banarasi sari* is an essential part of any marriage in the state.
- Gorakhpur is famous for its beautiful terracotta statues and handcraft cloths.
- Nizamabad is famous for black pottery.

ARTS AND CRAFTS: THE ARTISTIC SAGA OF UTTAR PRADESH

Is art and craft voiceless? Have you ever caressed the golden thread stylishly sewn through velvety muslin fabric? Indeed, our primary rendezvous with art does differ, but how it makes us feel, doesn't.

Exploring India through its artistic art and craft is an interesting journey. Different and of course, exotic! Fondly called as the 'Heartland of India,' it is lauded for its long living artistry. Stone-craft, pottery, Chikankari, Zari embroidery, glassware, textile printing and carpet weaving are few specialities of Uttar Pradesh.

Additionally, these artistic endeavours have years of history. For example, hand printing is the oldest craft of Uttar Pradesh. Its history dates back to 1714 AD when Farrukhabad the city famous for this craft was founded. Nawab Muhammad Khan Bangash had played a pivotal role in its establishment.

So, embark on a special journey with Uttar Pradesh Tour Packages and explore your own craving.

Do visit the famous Bari Bazar in Varanasi, famous for variety of Banarasi silk sarees and is one of the major manufacturing centres of handloom sarees in India.

Following are the main arts and handicrafts of Uttar Pradesh

Stone Craft

The Stone Craft of Uttar Pradesh has flourished due to the Muslim rulers of the state especially Mughals. The Taj Mahal in Agra is an excellent example of this craft. The other main cities include Agra, Varanasi and Fatehpur Sikri.

Thin marble slabs/stones are etched for hours to give them a meaningful shape and design. Intricate carvings are made by hour long chiselling. Walk through the narrow lanes of Agra and you will spot garden furniture, decorative items and many more similar crafted out of marbles.

Pottery

Pottery is popular throughout the state. However, potters of Meerut, Khurja and Hapur are more skilled in it. In fact, the history of Khurja pottery is nearly 600years old. Surahi, a vessel with long neck is the most popular item created through pottery. It is used in summers to keep the water cool.

These vessels are embellished with beautiful floral designs and patterns. Vibrant colours are used, mostly orange and yellow, against a plain white background. In spite of being fully handmade, these items are priced at very reasonable rates.

Chikankari

Chikankari or chikan work is synonymous to the city Lucknow. It is basically skilful embroidery done on fabricusing white thread. This intricate needle work owes its existence to Empress Nur Jahan, wife of Emperor Jahangir.

There are two main types of Chikan embroidery- flat and embossed. Flat embroidery involves simple sewing sans any loops or knots in threads. Bukhia and Katawa are the two famous styles under flat embroidery. Bukhia embroidery is basically stitches made in v shape while Katawa includes motifs cut from same fabric on which it is stitched to give an opaque appearance.

Zari Embroidery

Zari or Zardosi embroidery is famous in Varanasi. Rich golden threads are used to create beautiful designs and patterns on saris and other dress materials. Banarasi sarees are famous for their *zari* work. They are an indispensable part of Hindu marriages in North India.

The traditional thread work is done using real thread of gold and silver which makes the fabric expensive. Beads and stones are the other embellishments used institching. Some of the artisans also use synthetic thread instead of gold and silver. Such fabrics are heavy and bear an exquisite look. The fabric is used for making evening attires, bridal dresses and other occasional wears.

Glass Ware

Firozabad is famous for glassware especially the colourful glass bangles. Huge machines are used to create items like utensils, pots and myriad of toys. 'Firozabad' is also called as the 'City of bangles'.

Presumably, during ancient times foreign invaders had brought many glass items with them. They were later discarded and melted in a furnace. This marked the beginning of glass art in the city.

Beautiful chandeliers, jewelleries, decanters, cutlery sets and small trinkets are created using glass. The process involves basically heating of glass at high temperature. The matter softens and is then moulded into desirable shapes. The art also creates employment for women by engaging them in small-scale industries.

Carpet Weaving

Carpet weaving is another most famous handicraft practised in the state. Bhadohi city, about 40km away from Varanasi has excelled in this craft. History of carpet weaving in this city traces its roots to 16th century when the area was under the reign of Mughal Emperor Akbar.

Today it is the largest carpet manufacturing centre in the country and is also called as 'Carpet City'. You will find the finest of silk carpets sold in this area. They are adorned with delicate Persian patterns and look stunning.

Hand Printing

It is one of the oldest craft in the country. Farrukhabad city is lauded for it. Traditional patterns like *butis* (polka dots) and the 'tree of life' are made by hands on this fabric. The patterns are of dark colour, drawn against a soft coloured backdrop. Nowadays wooden blocks are also used to create these patterns.

'Paisley pattern' also famed as 'Mango' or 'Persian pickles' are the droplet shaped motif created using the *butis*. It is the second most popular pattern created by hand prints. It is commendable to see how the art has still managed to survive in this modern era of machines.

ARCHITECTURE OF UTTAR PRADESH

The Architecture of Uttar Pradesh is renowned for its variety of various religious monuments.

Hindu monuments

Temple in Barsana, near Mathura, dedicated to the worship of Radhaand Krishna.

Famous temples are Kashi Vishwanath Temple in Varanasi and Krishnajanmabhoomi in Mathura.

Islamic

Sultanates

Atala Masjid of Jaunpur shows a lot of influences of Hindu architecture. In fact, there is a clear resemblance of Hindu style of architecture, in the entire Masjid. The reason for such similarity is because the Atala Masjid is situated on the site of a temple of Atala Devi. Hence the Atala Masjid, Jaunpur also gets its name from this Hindu Temple.

Mughal

Buland Darwaza, the 54 mt. high entrance to Fatehpur Sikri complex

Uttar Pradesh has three World Heritage Sites: Taj Mahal, Agra Fort and the nearby Fatehpur Sikri. Allahabad Fort stands on the banks of the Yamuna near the confluence with the river Ganges. It is the largest fort built by Akbar.

Oudh

Lucknow, the capital of the state, has several beautiful historical monuments such as Bara Imambara and Chhota Imambara. It has also preserved the damaged complex of the Oudh-period British Resident's quarters, which are being restored.

Buddhist era

Most of the ancient buildings and structures at Sarnath

were damaged or destroyed by the Turks. However, amongst the ruins can be distinguished:

- The Dhamek Stupa; it is an impressive 128 feet high and 93 feet in diameter.
- The Dharmarajika Stupa is one of the few pre-Ashokan stupas remaining, although only the foundations remain.
- The Ashoka Pillar erected here, originally surmounted by the "Lion Capital of Asoka" (presently on display at the Sarnath Museum), was broken during Turk invasions but the base still stands at the original location.
- The Sarnath Archaeological Museum houses the famous Ashokan lion capital, which miraculously survived its 45-foot drop to the ground (from the top of the Ashokan Pillar), and became the National Emblem of India and national symbol on the Indian flag. The museum also houses a famous and refined Buddha-image of the Buddha in Dharmachakra-posture.

For Buddhists, Sarnath (or Isipatana) is one of four pilgrimage sites designated by Gautama Buddha, the other three being Kushinagar, Bodh Gaya, and Lumina.

KUMBH MELA

Kumbh Mela or Kumbha Mela is a mass Hindu pilgrimage of faith in which Hindus gather to bathe in a sacred or holy river. Traditionally, four fairs are widely recognized as the Kumbh Melas: the Haridwar Kumbh Mela, the Prayag Kumbh Mela, the Nashik-Trimbakeshwar Simhastha, and Ujjain Simhastha.

These four fairs are held periodically at one of the following places by rotation: Haridwar, Prayag (Prayaga), Nashik district (Nashik and Trimbak), and Ujjain. The main festival site is located on the banks of a river: the Ganges (*Ganga*) at Haridwar; the confluence (*Sangam*) of the Ganges and the Yamuna and the invisible Sarasvati at Prayag; the Godavari at Nashik; and the Shipra at Ujjain. Bathing in these rivers is thought to cleanse a person of all their sins.

At any given place, the Kumbh Mela is held once in 12 years. There is a difference of around 3 years between the Kumbh Melas at Haridwar and Nashik; the fairs at Nashik and Ujjain are celebrated in the same year or one year apart. The exact date is determined, as per Vikram Samvat calendar and the principles of Jyotisha, according to a combination of zodiac positions of the Jupiter, the Sun and the Moon. At Nashik and Ujjain, the Mela may be held while a planet is in Leo (Simha in Hindu astrology); in this case, it is also known as Simhastha. At Haridwar and Prayag, an *Ardha* ("Half") Kumbh Mela is held every sixth year; a *Maha* ("Great") Kumbh Mela occurs after 144 years.

The priests at other places have also claimed their local fairs to be Kumbh Melas. For example, the Mahamaham festival at Kumbakonam, held once in 12 years, is also portrayed as a Kumbh Mela.

The exact age of the festival is uncertain. According to medieval Hindu mythology, Lord Vishnu dropped drops of Amrita (the drink of immortality) at four places, while transporting it in a *kumbha* (pot). These four places are identified as the present-day sites of the Kumbh Mela. The name "Kumbh Mela" literally means "kumbha fair". It is known as "Kumbh" in Hindi (due to schwa deletion); in Sanskrit and some other Indian languages, it is more often known by its original name "Kumbha".

The festival is one of the largest peaceful gatherings in the world, and considered as the "world's largest congregation of religious pilgrims". There is no precise method of ascertaining the number of pilgrims, and the estimates of the number of pilgrims bathing on the most auspicious day may vary. An estimated 120 million people visited Maha Kumbh Mela in 2013 in Prayag over a two-month period, including over 30 million on a single day, on 10 February 2013 (the day of Mauni Amavasya). It has been inscribed on the UNESCO's Representative List of Intangible Cultural Heritage of Humanity,

Mythological origin

According to medieval Hindu mythology, the origin of the festival can be found in the ancient legend of *samudra manthan*. The legend tells of a battle between the Devas and Asuras for amrita, the drink of immortality. During *samudra manthan*, or churning of the ocean, amrita was produced and placed in a *kumbha* (pot). To prevent the asuras (malevolent beings) from seizing the amrita, a divine carrier flew away with the pot. In one version of the legend, the carrier of the *kumbha* is the divine physician Dhanavantari, who stops at four places where the Kumbh Mela is celebrated. In other re-tellings, the carrier is Garuda, Indra or Mohini, who spills the amrita at four places.

While several ancient texts, including the various Puranas, mention the *samudra manthan* legend, none of them mentions spilling of the amrita at four places. Neither do these texts mention the Kumbh Mela. Therefore, multiple scholars, including R. B. Bhattacharya, D. P. Dubey and Kama Maclean believe that the *samudra manthan* legend has been applied to the Kumbh Mela relatively recently, in order to show scriptural authority for it.

History

There are several references to river-side festivals in ancient Indian texts, but the exact age of the Kumbh Mela is uncertain. The Chinese traveler Xuanzang (Hiuen Tsang) describes a ritual organized by Emperor Shiladitya (identified with Harsha) at the confluence of two rivers, in the kingdom of Po-lo-ye-kia (identified with Prayaga). He also mentions that many hundreds took a bath at the confluence, to wash away their sins. According to some scholars, this is the earliest surviving historical account of the Kumbh Mela, which took place in present-day Prayag in 644 CE. However, Australian researcher Kama Maclean notes that the Xuanzang reference is about an event that happened every 5 years (and not 12 years), and might have been a Buddhist celebration (since, according to Xuanzang, Harsha was a Buddhist emperor).

A common conception, advocated by the akharas, is that Adi Shankara started the Kumbh Mela at Prayag in 8th century, to facilitate meeting of holy men from different regions. However, academics doubt the authenticity of this claim.

The Kumbh Mela of Haridwar appears to be the original Kumbh Mela, since it is held according to the astrological sign "Kumbha" (Aquarius), and because there are several references to a 12-year cycle for it. The earliest extant texts that contain the name "Kumbha Mela" are *Khulasat-ut-Tawarikh* (1695 CE) and *Chahar Gulshan* (1759 CE). Both these texts use the term "Kumbh Mela" to describe only Haridwar's fair, although they mention the similar fairs held in Prayag and Nashik district. The *Khulasat-ut-Tawarikh* lists the following melas: an annual mela and a Kumbh Mela every 12 years at Haridwar; a mela held at Trimbak when Jupiter enters Leo (that is, once in 12 years); and an annual mela held at Prayag in Magh. The Magh Mela of Prayag is probably the oldest among these, dating from the early centuries CE, and has been mentioned in several Puranas.However, its association with the Kumbha myth and the 12-year old cycle is relatively recent, probably dating back to the mid-19th century. D. P. Dubey notes that none of the ancient Hindu texts mention the Prayag fair as a "Kumbh Mela". Kama Maclean states that even early British records do not mention the name "Kumbh Mela" or the 12-year cycle for the Prayag fair. The first British reference to the Kumbh Mela in Prayag occurs only in an 1868 report, which mentions the need for increased pilgrimage and sanitation controls at the "Coomb fair" to be held in January 1870. According to Maclean, the Prayagwal Brahmin priests of Prayag adapted their annual Magh Mela to Kumbh legend, in order to increase the importance of their *tirtha*.

The Kumbh Mela at Ujjain began in the 18th century, when the Maratha ruler Ranoji Shinde invited ascetics from Nashik to Ujjain for a local festival. Like the priests at Prayag, the pandits of Nashik and Ujjain, competing with other places for a sacred status, may have adopted the Kumbh tradition for their pre-existing melas.

Until the East India Company rule, the Kumbh Melas were managed by the akharas (sects) of religious ascetics known as the sadhus. They collected taxes, and also carried out policing and judicial duties.

The sadhus were heavily militarized, and also participated in trade. The Melas were a scene of sectarian politics, which sometimes turned violent. The *Chahar Gulshan* states that the local sanyasis at Haridwar attacked the fakirs of Prayag who came to attend the Kumbh Mela there.

At the 1760 Kumbh Mela in Haridwar, a clash broke out between Shaivite Gosains and Vaishnavite Bairagis (ascetics), resulting in hundreds of deaths, with Vaishnavite forming most of the victims. A copper plate inscription of the Maratha Peshwa claims that 12,000 ascetics died in a clash between Shaivite *sanyasis* and Vaishnavite *bairagis* at the 1789 Nashik Kumbh Mela.

The dispute started over the bathing order, which indicated status of the *akharas*. At the 1796 Kumbh Mela in Haridwar, the Shaivites attacked and injured the Udasis for erecting a camp without their permission. In response, the Khalsa Sikhs accompanying the Udasis killed around 500 Gosains; the Sikhs lost around 20 men in the clash. The clashes subsided after the Company administration severely limited the trader-warrior role of the sadhus, who were increasingly reduced to begging.

Besides their religious significance, historically the Kumbh Melas were also major commercial events. Baptist missionary John Chamberlain, who visited the 1824 Ardh Kumbh Mela at Haridwar, stated that a large number of visitors came there for trade. He noted that the fair was attended by "multitudes of every religious order", including a large number of Sikhs. According to an 1858 account of the Haridwar Kumbh Mela by the British civil servant Robert Montgomery Martin, the visitors at the fair included people from a number of races and religions. Besides priests, soldiers, and religious mendicants, the fair was attended by several merchants, including horse traders from Bukhara, Kabul, Turkistan, Arabia and Persia. Several Hindu rajas, Sikh rulers and Muslim Nawabs visited the fair. A few Christian missionaries also preached at the Mela.

The Kumbh Melas played an important role in spread of the cholera outbreaks and pandemics. The British administrators made several attempts to improve the sanitary conditions at the Melas, but thousands of people died of cholera at these fairs until the mid-20th century.

Several stampedes have occurred at the Kumbh Melas. After an 1820 stampede at Haridwar that killed 485 people, the Company government took extensive infrastructure projects, including construction of new ghats and road widening, to prevent further stampedes. Since then Haridwar has experienced fewer deaths in stampedes: the next big stampede occurred in 1986, when 50 people were killed. Prayag has also experienced major stampedes, in 1840, 1906, 1954, 1986 and 2013. The deadliest of these was the 1954 stampede, which left 800 people dead.

Places

Traditionally, the fairs at the following four sites are recognized as Kumbh Melas: Prayag (Allahabad), Haridwar, Trimbak-Nashik and Ujjain. The Kumbh Mela in the Nashik district was originally held at Trimbak, but after a 1789 clash between Vaishnavites and Saivitesover precedence of bathing, the Maratha Peshwa shifted the Vaishnavites' bathing place to Ramkund in Nashik city. The Shaivites continue to regard Trimbak as the proper location.

Priests at other places have also attempted to boost the status of their *tirtha* by adapting the Kumbh legends. The places whose festivals have been claimed as "Kumbh Mela" include Varanasi, Vrindavan, Tirumakudal Narsipur, Kumbhakonam (Mahamaham) and Rajim (Rajim Kumbh). Even Tibet has hosted a festival claimed to be a Kumbh Mela.

Dates

The Kumbh Mela occurrences follow the Hindu calendar, as follows:

- The Kumbh Mela (sometimes specifically called *Purna Kumbh* or "full Kumbha"), occurs every 12 years at a given site.
- Ardh Kumbh ("Half Kumbh") Mela occurs between the two Purna Kumbha Melas at Prayag and Haridwar.
- The Maha Kumbh occurs after 12 Purna Kumbh Melas i.e. every 144 years.

The Kumbh Mela at Prayag is celebrated after approximately 3 years of Kumbh Mela at Haridwar. There is a difference of around 3 years between the Kumbh Festivals at Prayag and Nashik. Kumbh at Nashik and Ujjain are celebrated in the same year or one year apart.

Attendance

According to *The Imperial Gazetteer of India*, an outbreak of cholera occurred at the 1892 Mela at Haridwar leading to the rapid improvement of arrangements by the authorities and to the formation of Haridwar Improvement Society. In 1903 about 400,000 people are recorded as attending the fair. During the 1954 Kumbh Mela stampede at Prayag, around 500 people were killed, and scores were injured. Ten million people gathered at Haridwar for the Kumbh on 14 April 1998.

In 2001, more than 40 million gathered on the busiest of its 55 days.

According to the Mela Administration's estimates, around 70 million people participated in the 45-day Ardha Kumbh Mela at Prayag in 2007.

The 2001 Kumbh Mela at Prayag (Prayag) was estimated by the authorities to have attracted between 30 and 70 million people.The estimated attendance for the 2013 Prayag Kumbh Mela was 120 million.

The ritual

One of the major events of Kumbh Mela is the Peshwai Procession, which marks the arrival of the members of an akhara or sect of sadhus at the Kumbh Mela. The major event of the festival is ritual bathing at the banks of the river in whichever town Kumbh Mela being held:Ganga in Haridwar, Godavari in Nasik, Kshipra in Ujjain and Sangam (confluence of Ganga, Yamuna and mythical Saraswati) in Allahabad (Prayag). Nasik has registered maximum visitors to 75 million. Other activities include religious discussions, devotional singing, mass feeding of holy men and women and the poor, and religious assemblies where doctrines are debated and standardised. Kumbh Mela is the most sacred of all the pilgrimages. Thousands of holy men and women attend, and the auspiciousness of the festival is in part attributable to this. The sadhus are seen clad in saffron sheets with Vibhuti ashes dabbed on their skin as per the requirements of ancient traditions. Some, called *naga sanyasis*, may not wear any clothes even in severe winter. The right to be naga, or naked, is considered a sign of separation from the material world.

The order of entering the water is fixed, with the Juna, the Niranjani and Mahanirvani akharas preceding.

After visiting the Kumbh Mela of 1895, Mark Twain wrote:

"It is wonderful, the power of a faith like that, that can make multitudes upon multitudes of the old and weak and the young and frail enter without hesitation or complaint upon such incredible journeys and endure the resultant miseries without repining. It is done in love, or it is done in fear; I do not know which it is. No matter what the impulse is, the act born of it is beyond imagination, marvelous to our kind of people, the cold whites. "

Darshan

Darshan, or respectful visual exchange, is an important part of the Kumbh Mela. People make the pilgrimage to the Kumbh Mela specifically to observe and experience both the religious and secular aspects of the event. Two major groups that participate in the Kumbh Mela include the Sadhus (Hindu holy men) and pilgrims. Through their continual yogic practices the Sadhus articulate the transitory aspect of life. Sadhus travel to the Kumbh Mela to make themselves available to much of the Hindu public. This allows members of the Hindu public to interact with the Sadhus and to take "darshan." They are able to "seek instruction or advice in their spiritual lives." Darshan focuses on the visual exchange, where there is interaction with a religious deity and the worshiper is able to visually "'drink' divine power." The Kumbh Mela is arranged in camps that give Hindu worshipers access to the Sadhus. The darshan is important to the experience of the Kumbh Mela and because of this worshipers must be careful so as to not displease religious deities. Seeing of the Sadhus is carefully managed and worshipers often leave tokens at their feet.

Kumbh Mela in media

Kumbh Mela has received extensive media coverage, with several documentaries and films based on it.

Kumbh Mela has been theme for many a documentaries, including *Kings with Straw Mats* (1998) directed by Ira Cohen, *Kumbh Mela: The Greatest Show on Earth* (2001) directed by Graham Day, *Short Cut to Nirvana: Kumbh Mela* (2004) directed by Nick Day and produced by "Maurizio Benazzo", *Kumbh Mela: Songs of the River* (2004) by Nadeem Uddin, *Invocation, Kumbh Mela* (2008), *Kumbh Mela: Walking with the Nagas* (2011), *Amrit: Nectar of Immortality* (2012) directed by Jonas Scheu and Philipp Eyer, *Inside the Mahakumbh* (2013) by the National Geographic Channel and *Kumbh Mela 2013: living with Mahatiagi* (2013) by the Ukrainian Religious Studies Project Ahamot.

Indian and foreign news media have covered the Kumbh Mela regularly. On 18 April 2010, a popular American morning show *CBS News Sunday Morning* extensively covered Haridwar's Kumbh Mela, calling it "*The Largest Pilgrimage on Earth*". On 28 April 2010, BBC reported an audio and a video report on Kumbh Mela, titled "*Kumbh Mela 'greatest show on earth.*"

Young siblings getting separated at the Kumbh Mela were once a recurring theme in Hindi movies. *Amrita Kumbher*

Sandhane, a 1982 Bengali feature film directed by Dilip Roy, also documents the Kumbh Mela. On 30 September 2010, the Kumbh Mela featured in the second episode of the Sky One TV series "An Idiot Abroad" with Karl Pilkington visiting the festival.

In 2015, the Nashik Kumbha Mela became a technology savvy festival due to a collaboration of the city government with MIT Media Lab and Kumbhathon Foundation in Nashik. This received significant media coverage in Wall Street Journal, BBC and Guardian. The Nashik Kumbh Mela was considered one of the most peaceful and successful as there were no stampedes, no epidemic or separated families reported. Well known photographer John Werner captured the Kumbh Mela and released the photographs under creative commons.

FESTIVALS

Religious practices are as much an integral part of everyday life, and a very public affair, as they are in the rest of India. Therefore, not surprisingly, many festivals are religious in origin, although several of them are celebrated irrespective of caste and creed.

Among the most important Hindu festivals are Diwali, Holi and Dussehra, which are also observed with equal fervour by Jains. Ten days of Ramlila takes place during the period of navratri and on the 10th day, epithet of Raavan is burnt with great fervour. Durga puja is also observed in many parts of the state during navratri. Bârah Wafâm□, Eid, Bakreed and Birthdate of Imam Ali ibn Abitalib are recognised official Muslim religious festivals. Moharram, though the day of Ashura is official holiday but Shiites consider it as a day of mourning and not a festival as some people believe. Mahavir Jayanti is celebrated by Jains, Buddha Jayanti by Buddhists, Guru Nanak Jayanti by Sikhs and Christmas by the Christians.Other festivals include Ram navami, Chhath puja, Krishna-janmashtami, Mahashivratri, etc.

Karva Chauth: This festival falls on nine days after Dussehra, on the fourth day of the dark fortnight of Kartika.

Karva Chauth is held by married Hindu woman for the safety and prosperity of their husbands. The day is spent in complete fasting till the rise of the moon and it is worshipped by women. Four days later, is the festival of Ahoi Astami, when women fast and pray for the welfare of their children. Followed five days later, by a series of festivals culminating in Diwali, the festival of lights on Kartika Amavasya.

Annakoot is celebrated which is devoted to feasting and Govardhan puja in the evening and rounded up next day by Bhaiya Dooj when sisters apply vermilion tika (auspicious mark) on the forehead of their brothers who reward them with money. On Dooj weapons, pen and inkpot are also worshipped.

Shitla Ashtami, which falls on eight day after Holi, is devoted to the goddess of small-pox, followed by Ram Navami on Chaitra Sudi Navami, commemorating the birth of Lord Rama; Baisakhi Purnima, a big bathing day; Bargadee Amavasya in Jaistha Dussehra, another great bathing day; Guru Purnima in Asadh when Vyas Puja is held and Nag Panchami dedicated to the worship of the Snake God, Shesha.

Janmashtami is the most important Hindu festival celebrating the birthday of Lord Krishna. This festival is followed by Hartalika Teej, Ganesh Chaturthi, Anant Chaturdashi, and Pitra Visarjan Amavasya devoted to making of oblations to the pitras (dead ancestors) and is called Pitra Paksha.

Bharat Milap which is celebrated during the month of October or November is performed at Nati Imli on the day following Vijayadashmi (Dusshera). It pertains to the episode of the return of Lord Rama to Ayodhya after 14 years of exile, and his reunion with his brother Bharat. Just as the last rays of the setting sun touch the stage, the performance takes barely three minutes to enact.

Another episode from Ram Lila pertains to Shoorpnakha, demon king Ravana's sister. This festival is held on the 4th night of Kartika at Chetganj. It lasts almost the whole night. The 'Kalia Daman' episode from 'Krishna Lila' is celebrated in November on the Tulsi ghat. Shivratri is celebrated on the 14th day of Phalgun. 'Ganga-Dussehra' and 'Nirjala Ekadashi' fall on the 10th day of bright half of Jayestha. It is believed that Ganga waters reached Haridwar this day in the remote past. The next day, is the day of fasting for all the devotees. Panchkoshi Parikarma is another famous pilgrimage. It is held in the month of Vaisakh, circumambulation of 'Kashi-Dharma Kshetra'.

MUSLIM FESTIVALS

The most solemn and colourful Muslim function held in the state is Muharram, commemorating the martyrdom of Imam Hussain, the grandson of the Holy Prophet. In all cities and towns Muslims take out impressive processions of colourfully decorated tazias, replicas of the martyr's tomb at Karbala.

The most solemn and impressive Muharram is observed in Lucknow, where gold and silver replicas of old Nawabi times are brought out and men beat their breasts in mourning constantly until blood oozes out.

The two Imambaras and Shah Najaf are beautifully illuminated for two days. An impressive event is a fire-walking feat held in one of the Imambaras. After the burial of the tazias on the tenth day, a gathering of mourners in utter darkness is held, known as Majlis Sham-i-Ghariban, one of the most soul-stirring events among Muharram observances.

The other occasions of religious importance for Muslims are Id-ul-fitr, Ramzan (a month devoted to fasting), Chehlum, Bara Wafat, Shah-i-Barat and Id-uz-Zuha.

Festivals of almost all the religions are celebrated in U.P. The composite culture of the State is famous all over India. Various communities celebrate as many as 40 festivals with gaiety and complete communal harmony.

Sheetla Ashtami, Raksha Bandhan, Vaishakhi Purnima, Ganga Dashahara, Naag Panchami, Krishna Janmashtami, Ram Navami, Ganesha Chaturthi, Vijaya Dashmi, Deepawali, Kartik Purnima, Makar Sankranti, Vasant Panchami, Shivaratri and Holi are the main festivals of the Hindus.

I'd, Moharram, Bakr-I'd, Barawafat and Shab-e-Barat are

the major Muslim festivals. New Years Day, Good-Friday, Easter and Christmas are the prominent festivals of the Christians. Buddha Purnima for Buddhists, Mahavir Jayanti for Jains, the birthday of Guru Nanak, Martyr's day of Guru Teg Bahadur and Vaishakhi are the famous festivals of the people of Sikh faith.

About 2,250 fairs are held every year in Uttar Pradesh. The largest number of fairs are held in Mathura (86), followed by Kanpur and Hamirpur (79), Jhansi (78), Agra (72), and Fatehpur (70).

UTTAR PRADESH FAMOUS FESTIVALS

Eid-ul-Fitr : This festival, which occurs at the end of the month of Ramzan, is the gayest and falls on the first day of the tenth month of the Hijrah calendar.

Eid-ul-Adha : Also known as Bakrid or Eid ul Adha, the festival of Eid Ul Zuha is one of the most important in the Muslim calendar. It is observed on the tenth day of the twelfth month in the Muslim calendar. The sanctity of the day- and the period preceding it- makes this a popular time for undertaking the pilgrimage (the Haj) to Mecca.

Muharrum : The most solemn and colourful Muslim function held in the state is Muharram, commemorating the martyrdom of Imam Hussain, the grandson of the Holy Prophet. In all cities and towns Muslims take out impressive processions of colourfully decorated tazias, replicas of the martyr's tomb at Karbala. The most solemn and impressive Muharram is observed in Lucknow, where gold and silver replicas of old Nawabi times are brought out and men beat their breasts in mourning constantly until blood oozes out. The two Imambaras and Shah Najaf are beautifully illuminated for two days. An impressive event is a fire-walking feat held in one of the Imambaras. After the burial of the tazias on the tenth day, a gathering of mourners in utter darkness is held, known as Majlis Sham-i-Ghariban, one of the most soul-stirring events among Muharram observances.

Diwali : The Hindu Festival of Diwali is celebrated with great vigour over here. The state wears a vibrant colour throughout the Diwali festival. The festival Diwali celebrates the homecoming of Rama with firecrackers and the lighting of earthen lamps. Ramlila performances during Dussehra commemorate this joyous event as well. Traditionally the characters of Rama, Sita, Lakshmana, Shatrughan and Bharat are played by Brahmin boys who are trained by the liladhari, the leader of the troupe.

Taj Mahotsav : The Taj Mahotsav is a nonstop 10 day carnival held annually at Shilpgram, near Tajmahal. With the wondrous Taj Mahal serving as the backdrop for the annual festival, the Taj Mahotsav is celebrated in the month of February. The Taj festival is a culturally vibrant platform that brings together the finest Indian crafts and cultural nuances.

The impressive festival commences with a spectacular procession inspired by Mughal splendour. Bedecked elephants and camels, drum beaters, folk artists and master craftsmen together recreate the glorious past of the Mughals. From folk music, shayari (poetry), classical dance performances, elephant and camel rides to games and a food festival, the event is a celebration of traditional Indian art forms and crafts. The main events of Taj Mahal festival include classical dance performances by leading dance exponents and musical recitals by maestros, apart from display of various craft products and cultural shows.

Bateshwar Fair : Situated at a distance of 70 km. from Agra on the banks of river Yamuna, Bateshwar is an important spiritual and cultural centre. The place is named after the presiding deity of the region, Bateshwar Mahadeo and has 108 temples dedicated to the gods and goddesses of the Hindu pantheon.

During the months of Oct. & Nov. a large fair is organized from Shashthi of Kartik month to Panchami of Agrahayan month. Devotees congregate here in large numbers to worship Lord Shiva and take holy dips in river Yamuna. A livestock fair is also organized and owners and buyers conduct serious business combined with the gaiety of a market place.

Rambarat : The marriage procession of Sri Ram, is held every year during Ramlila celebrations at Agra. Every year a new locale of the town is chosen as Janakpuri, which is elaborately decorated to perform the royal wedding. The Rambarat (marriage procession) starts from Lala Channomaiji Id Baradari for Janakpuri passing through different parts of the town. The barat is a large procession of Jhankis followed by the swaroops of Ram-Lakshman mounted on elephants.

Kailash Fair : Held at Kailash. 12 km. from Agra during the months of Aug.-Sept. It is a major fair celebrated in honour of Lord Shiva who is believed to have appeared here in the form of a stone lingam.

Water Sports Festival : Water sports festival, Allahabad is an event packed with adventure thrills of kayaking, canoeing and other water sport activities. Organised at Allahabad every year, the event is an opportunity to indulge in water sport activities of varied nature.

Ram Lila : Janmashtami, the birth of Lord Krishna is celebrated with great devotion in the August/September months, on the Ashtami of Krishna Paksh or the 8th day of the dark fortnight in the month of Bhadon, in the whole of north India. Temples and homes are beautifully decorated and lit. An attractive feature of the celebrations are cribs & other decorations depicting stories of Lord Krishna's childhood. There are five main "jhankis" of Janmashtami which depict the entire sequence of events from Lord Krishna's birth to his being discovered in Gokul. The "jhankis" include the birth of Krishna in jail, Vasudev carrying Krishna to safety across the river Yamuna amidst thunder and lightning, Vasudev's return to the jail, Kansa killing Yashoda's daughter and finally the little Krishna in the cradle in Gokul. "Jhankis" are created out of dolls dressed up as kids, men and women with lehangas, chunnis, dhotis & kurtas. Raslila of every type are also performed - Janmalila, Shankarlila, Putnalila and Naglila. In the evening bhajans are sung which end at midnight, the auspicious moment when Lord Krishna was born. Thereafter arti is done, prasad distributed and flowers showered on the idol.

Ram Navmi Mela : Ayodhya, the holy city of the sacred pilgrim centre of Hindus plays host to the Ramnavmi Festival in the month of April. Thousands of worshippers gather to venerate the Lord at Kanak Bhawan.

Sravan Jhula Mela : This mela celebrates the playful spirit of the deities. On the third day of the second half of Shravan, images of the deities (specially of Rama, Lakshman & Sita) are placed in swings in the temples. They are also taken to Maniparvat, where the idols are made to swing from the branches of the trees. Later the deities are brought back to temples. The Mela lasts till the end of the month of Shravan.

Parikramas : Ayodhya is perhaps the most noted place in the northern India where parikramas are undertaken by Hindu Pilgrims. These are circumambulations of important religious places and are of varying duration, shortest being the `Antargrahi Parikrama which has to be completed within a day. After taking a dip in the Saryu, the devotee commences the parikarma from the Nageshwarnath temple and passes through Rama Ghat, Sita Kund, Manipuravata and Brahma Kund, finally terminating at Kanak Bhawan.

Then there is the `Panchkoshi Parikrama circuit of 10 miles, which touches Chakratirtha, Nayaghat, Ramghat, Saryubagh, Holkar-ka-pura, Dashrathkund, Jogiana, Ranopali, Jalpa Nala and Mahtabagh. On the way the people pay homage to deities in the shrines which are situated on the route. The `Chaturdashkoshi Parikrama constitutes a circular journey of 28 miles made once a year on the occasion of Akshainaumi, which is completed within 24 hours

Ramayana Mela : A huge fair is held in Ayodhya on Ram Navami day, where thousands of devotees gather to celebrate this festival. Processions accompanied by splendid floats of Rama, his wife Sita, his brother Lakshman and his monkey-general, Hanuman are carried out with great zest.

Ramnavmi : Ram Navami commemorates the birth of Lord Rama, the seventh reincarnation of Lord Vishnu. Ram Navami is celebrated with religious fervour. On this day, people observe a fast. In all the Ram mandirs, Aarti and Pooja are performed during the noon hours, the time of Lord Rama's birth. On Ram Navami day, all the Ram temples are beautifully decorated the idols of Lord Ram, his wife Sita and his brother Lakshman are adorned with new clothes, jewellery and flowers.

Navaratri : The festival of Dassera, is one of the fascinating festivals of India and is celebrated with joy and enthusiasm for ten continuous days. The first nine nights are spent in the worship of goddess Durga and hence these nights are known as "Navaratri". This festival falls in the month of Ashwin (September / October). The tenth day of the Dassera day is in honour of Durga Devi. The tribal communities also worship Durga as the presiding deity of Navaratri. The farmers invoke her blessings because this festival coincides with the period of rest and leisure after their strenuous work in the fields. The farmers with her blessings wait with tremendous hopes for a bountiful harvest.

Vijayadashmi : The tenth day of the Dassera day is in honour of Durga Devi and celebrated as vijayadasami.. The tribal communities also worship Durga as the presiding deity of Navaratri. The farmers invoke her blessings because this festival coincides with the period of rest and leisure after their strenuous work in the fields. The farmers with her blessings wait with tremendous hopes for a bountiful harvest.

Amavasya Fair : Held everymonth on Amavasya day in Chitrakoot.

Ayurveda-Janshi Mahotsava : Jhansi is one of the major centers for production of Ayurvedic medicines in U.P. Hence the Jhansi festival aims at highlighting the Ayurvedic system of healing and uses of Ayurveda for general well-being. Clubbed with Handicraft fair and traditional folk performances by regional artists, the Jhansi Mahotsav becomes a complete celebration of art, craft and culture of the Bundelkhand region. The festival also aims at projecting U.P. as the most accessible and approachable destination for attracting people for Health tourism.

Kapilvastu Buddha Mahotsava : Celebrated every year from 29 Dec. to 31 Dec. Fair is also organised on Budhpoornima.

Kartik Poornima/Srawan Mela : Varanasi is the land of festivals. Kartik Poornima celebrated in the month of Nov.-Dec., is the sacred day, when the ghats of Varanasi come alive with thousands of brightly lit earthen lamps. Visitors throng in large numbers to watch this spectacular event, famous as Dev Deepawali.

Magh Mela : Magh Mela is the annual version of the Kumbh Mela and considered as the mini Kumbh, celebrated at the holy Sangam at Allahabad. The event starts from Makar Sankranti and ends at Maha Shivratri, during which several dates are deemed as auspicious for taking holy dips in the Sangam.

Buddha Poornima : Buddha Poornima, which falls on the full moon night in the month of Vaisakha (either in April or May), commemorates the birth anniversary of Lord Buddha, founder of Buddhism, one of the oldest religions in the world. A large fair is held at Sarnath and the relics of the Buddha are taken out for a public display on a procession, on this day.

Lucknow Mahotsava : The Lucknow Festival held in the months of November-December captures the undying elegance and splendours of Awadh, now Lucknow. A brilliant showcase of the arts, crafts, and above all the heavenly cuisine of this land, the festival is a once-in-a-lifetime experience. This festival celebrates Lucknow's living culture. The capital city of Uttar Pradesh is alight with excitement during this ten day long event. Colourful processions, traditional dramas, Kathak dances in the style of the famous Lucknow Gharana, sarangi and sitar recitals alongwith ghazals, qawalis and thumri create a festive atmosphere. Exciting events like ekka races, kite flying, cock fighting and other traditional village games recreate an atmosphere of Awadh's nawabi days.

Ganga Mahotsav : Varanasi is a city of festivals, which is perched on the edge of time along the banks of an everflowing river. Every year at Varanasi, devouts and visitors, alike, celebrate the ancient glory of the Ganga. Every year a festive experience like none other awaits you at Ganga Festival at Varanasi.

Baudh Mahotsava : It is celebrated in the month of December by the Uttar Pradesh tourism department in various cities of the state.

Ramlila Ramnagar : Ramnagar, 15 km. from Varanasi presents the Ramlila (traditional enactment of the mythological text 'Ramayana') in the most traditional style. The performances last for 31 days. Hundreds of sandhus called the 'Ramayanis' come to watch and recite the Ramayana. Permanent structures are built and spaces designated to represent the main locales of the story *i.e.* Ashok Vatika, Janakpuri, Panchvati, Lanka etc., transforming the whole town into a vast Ramlila ground.

The audience moves along with the performers with every episode, to the next locale. The greatest attraction is the austere character of the Ramlila. To this day electric lights, mikes and loudspeakers are not used, whereas the average audience is rarely less than ten thousand on any day.

Nag Nathaiya : The Tulsi Ghat at Varanasi is die venue for the 20 day long Krishna Leela celebration, of which Nag-Nathaiya Leela, one of the episodes is extremely famous. Lord Krishna enacted by an artist, jumps into the river as the play reaches climax and emerges on the serpent hood of Shesh Nag. Lakhs of people gather on the ghats of Ganga to witness this special enactment.

Dhrupad Mela : Dhrupad Mela march A 5-day music festival of Dhrupad is perfomed by renowned artistes at Tulsi Ghat. It is very popular among foreign tourists.

Sankat Mochan Music Festival : Janmotsav of Lord Hanuman is celebrated at Sankat Mochan Temple for 5 days with the cultural and musical programmes by artists from all over India.

Kartik Poornima/Dev Deepawali : At the occasion of Kartik Poornima the ghats of Varanasi come alive with thousands of diyas (earthen lamps) lit together. This spectacular event famous as the Dev-Deepawali is celebrated on the 15th day after Diwali, as a tribute to river Ganga by the people of Varanasi.

Holi : Holi heralds the beginning of spring and is celebrated with great enthusiasm all over India. According to a legend, Hiranya Kashyap, the demon who ruled over 'Sapta Deep' believed himself to be more powerful than God. He contemplated killing his youngest son Prahlad, an ardent devotee of Lord Vishnu after he refused to worship him as God. Holika, the demon's sister who possessed a divine, garment to protect her from fire, agreed to enter the burning pyre with Prahlad in her lap but got burnt herself.

Holi thus signifies the triumph of good over evil and is marked by grand festivities all over India and particularly in the Braj area where it is celebrated with great gaiety and fervour. It is believed that Lord Krishna, an incarnation of Lord Vishnu, in human form played holi with the Gopi's (cowherd maids) in the ancient past.

Keeping this tradition alive in Braj, Holi celebrations last for more than a week and are marked by people sprinkling coloured water & smearing coloured powder on each other. The playful teasing of the Gopis by the Gopas (cowherd boys) is enacted by groups of men and women through special Holi songs and dances, called Rasiya.

Janmashtami : Janmashtami, the birthday of Shri Krishna is celebrated with great pomp and splendour throughout Braj. The Raaslila is enacted recreating the many legends of Shri Krishna's life - his exploits and his amorous dalliances with the gopies. Ceremonies in the temples at midnight include the bathing of the image of infant Krishna which is then placed in a silver cradle. Songs of devotion are sung and toys offered for the amusement of the divine child. Thousands gather to offer their prayers and Mathura is astir with their devotion and celebrations.

Kampil Fair : Kampilya called Kampil today, is a village in tehsil Kasganj of Etah district, situated on the banks of the

Ganga. During the epic period it was the capital of King Drupad, the father of the Queen Draupadi, wife of the five Pandava's of Mahabharat. It was the birth place of the 13th tirthaiikar Brahlan Vimal Nath and was graced by the visit of Lord Mahavir. The neighbouring ruins and mounds contain the relics and sculptures of Jain period. Every year a Jain Mela is held for five days in the month of March thronged by Jain devouts.

Deva Mela : The annual urs of Haji Waris Ali Shah is celebrated during Oct.-Nov. months at Deva 10 km. from Barabanki. This fair attracts pilgrims from as far as Pakistan and the middle east countries. The shrine of the Sufi Saint is much revered by Muslim pilgrims all over the world.

FAIRS AND FESTIVALS IN UTTAR PRADESH

The state of Uttar Pradesh is reflective of true secular spirit. Festivals of different communities are celebrated in the state of Uttar Pradesh with a lot of pomp and grandeur. It embodies the rich and composite cultural heritage of our country.

A visit to the Fairs and Festivals of Uttar Pradesh gives us a picture of true communal harmony. It is indeed a rainbow land where Holi and Muharram give equal joy to the people. One will be amazed to know that each year Uttar Pradesh is the venue of as many as 2250 fairs.

You are at complete liberty to visit the state of Uttar Pradesh at any time because the celebrations in the state never seem to end. One or the other of the festivals belonging to different communities is celebrated in this land with equal ceremonial elegance and splendor at all times of the year. There is festivity in the air always.

Fairs and Festivals of Uttar Pradesh

With its 40 grand festivals and about 2,250 fairs, Uttar Pradesh is considered among the most colourful state of the country. All the occasions are celebrated with enthusiasm and excitement. These are the occasions when artists exhibit their talent in the most professional manner. Gymnasts, snake charmers, jugglers and the magicians are common sight of the fairs in Uttar Pradesh.

Festivals like Raksha Bandhan, Vaishakhi Purnima, Dussehra, Krishna Janmashtami, Ram Navami, Ganesha Chaturthi, Deepawali, Shivaratri, Holi, Eid, Shab-e-Barat, New Year's Day, Christmas, Buddha Purnima, Guru Nanak's Birthday etc. are celebrated in Uttar Pradesh with warm communal harmony like other parts of India. Apart from these major festivals (national festivals), Uttar Pradesh is visited for several unique fairs and celebrations.

The Kumbh and the Ardh Kumbh

These fairs are organised every twelve and six years in Haridwar. In India, the Kumbh and Ardh Kumbh are also celebrated in Prayag, Nasik and Ujjain. Lakhs of pilgrims, sages and saints flock to these Tirathas (pilgrimages) to celebrate this divine event. They take dips in the holy rivers considering the water as Amrit (nectar). These much awaited fairs are perfect blends of religious and social features of the Hindu culture.

Ramlila

Ramlila is famous for the enactment of the story of Lord Rama, on the basis of the holy epic Ramcharitmanas (written by the great saint Tulsidas). In several places, it is linked with Vijayadashmi celebrations on the occasion of Dussehra in late September or early October and also with Ram Navami, the birthday of Lord Rama.

Ram Navmi Mela

Ayodhya hosts this grand festival on the occasion of Lord Rama's birthday. The festival is celebrated in the month of April. Numerous devotees gather to venerate the Lord at Kanak Bhawan.

Shravan Jhula Mela

As the name suggests, the fair is organised in the month of Shravan according to the Hindu calender. The images or idols of Lord Rama, Goddess Sita and Lakshman are taken to Mani Parvat, where these are made to swing from the branches of the trees. The fair lasts till the end of the month of Shravan.

Jhanda Fair

This fair is organised at Dehradun as a tribute to Guru Ram Rai, the Sikh Guru. He once visited Dehradun in the year 1699 when he built a gurudwara (Guru Ram Rai Darbar) and hoisted his flag (Jhanda). This fair marks this event. A huge fair is held every year in the month of March (on the sixth day after Holi) and a flag is unfurled at Jhanda Chowk.

Tapkeshwar Fair

Tapkeshwar Shiv Temple is located at 6 km from Dehradun. A fair, dedicated to Lord Shiva, is held here on Shivratri every year.

Barsana Holi

Barsana or 'Latthmar' Holi is celebrated at Barsasa (48 km from Mathura). As the legend goes, Lord Krishna used to visit Barsana with his friends (Gopas) to play Holi with his beloved Radha and her friends (Gopis). While playing, the gopas were chased by the gopis with 'Lathis' (bamboo) in their hands, thus giving rise to the 'Latthmar Holi' of Barsana. The festival is celebrated with coloured powder and coloured water at the Ladliji temple, dedicated to Sri Radha Rani.

After Barsana, Holi is also celebrated at Baldeo (the town named after Balram; 20 km from Mathura) and Nandgaon (7 km from Barsana).

Kampil Fair, Kampil

A Jain fair is organised at Kampil or Kampilya village in tehsil Kasganj of Etah district. The city was once the capital of King Drupad (father of Queen Draupadi of the epic Mahabharata). The renowned town is known as the birth place of the 13th tirthankar Brahlan Vimal Nath and was once visited by Lord Mahavir. A five day fair is organised here on the banks of River Ganga in the month of March.

Taj Mahotsava

This is a grand festival organised in Agra (along the river Yamuna) by UP Tourism to pay a tribute to the legendary craftsmen of Uttar Pradesh. The festival exhibits the arts, crafts, culture and cuisine of the Braj area.

Yoga Festival at Varanasi & Allahabad

This is a recent addition to the state culture. It is organised to promote the unparalleled art of meditation and Yoga that has heavily influenced the India and world. Great sages and Yogis teach the perfect way to find peace of mind and solace without corrupting the soul.

10

Education

EDUCATION IN UTTAR PRADESH

Uttar Pradesh has a long tradition of education, although historically it was primarily confined to the elite class and religious schools.Sanskrit-based learning formed the major part of education from the Vedic to the Gupta periods. As cultures travelled through the region they brought their bodies of knowledge with them, adding Pali, Persian and Arabic scholarship to the community.

These formed the core of Hindu-Buddhist-Muslim education until the rise of British colonialism. The present schools-to-university system of education owes its inception and development in the state (as in the rest of the country) to foreign Christian missionaries and the British colonial administration.

Schools in the state are either managed by the government or by private trusts. Hindi is used as a medium of instruction in most of the schools except those affiliated to the CBSE or the Council for ICSE boards. Under the 10+2+3 plan, after completing secondary school, students typically enroll for 2 years in a junior college, also known as pre-university, or in schools with a higher secondary facility affiliated with the Uttar Pradesh Board of High School and Intermediate Education or a central board. Students choose from one of three streams, namely liberal arts, commerce, or science. Upon completing the required coursework, students may enroll in general or professional degree programs.

Central Drug Research Institute, an autonomous multidisciplinary research institute

Uttar Pradesh has more than 45 universities, including 5 central universities, 28 state universities, 8 deemed universities, 2 IITs in Varanasi and Kanpur, 1 IIM in Lucknow, 1 NIT in Allahabad, 2 IIITs, 1 National Law University in Lucknow and several polytechnics, engineering colleges and industrial training institutes. Prestigious institutes like the Aligarh Muslim University, Sanjay Gandhi Postgraduate Institute of Medical Sciences, Indian Institute of Technology (Kanpur), Indian Institute of Technology (BHU), the Indian Institute of Management (Lucknow), Motilal Nehru National Institute of Technology (Allahabad), Indian Institute of Information Technology (Allahabad), Indian Institute of Information Technology (Lucknow), University Institute of Engineering and Technology, Kanpur, King George's Medical University, Dr. Ram Manohar Lohiya National Law University and the Harcourt Butler Technical University are known worldwide for their quality education and research in their respective fields. The presence of such institutions provides the students of the state with ample opportunities for higher education.

Other universities in the state include Banaras Hindu University, University of Allahabad, University of Lucknow, Uttar Pradesh University of Medical Sciences, Chandra Shekhar

Azad University of Agriculture and Technology, Chaudhary Charan Singh University, Dr. B. R. Ambedkar University, Chhatrapati Shahu Ji Maharaj University, Dr. Ram Manohar Lohia Avadh University, Madan Mohan Malaviya University of Technology, Gautam Buddha University, Deen Dayal Upadhyay Gorakhpur University, Indian Veterinary Research Institute Bareilly, IMT Ghaziabad, Dr. Ram Manohar Lohia Institute of Medical Sciences, Dr. A.P.J. Abdul Kalam Technical University, M.J.P. Rohilkhand University, Bundelkhand University, Narendra Dev University of Agriculture and Technology, Babasaheb Bhimrao Ambedkar University, Veer Bahadur Singh Purvanchal University, Bhartendu Academy of Dramatic Arts, Siddharth University, Allahabad State University and Khwaja Moinuddin Chishti Urdu, Arabi~Farsi University.

The Integral University, a state level institution, was established by the Uttar Pradesh Government to provide education in different technical, applied science, and other disciplines. The Central Institute of Higher Tibetan Studies was founded as an autonomous organisation by the national ministry of culture. Jagadguru Rambhadracharya Handicapped University is the only university established exclusively for the disabled in the world. A large number of Indian scholars are educated at different universities in Uttar Pradesh. Notable scholars who were born, worked or studied in the geographic area of the state include Harivansh Rai Bachchan, Motilal Nehru, Harish Chandra and Indira Gandhi.

HISTORY OF EDUCATION

The region of Uttar Pradesh had a long tradition of learning, although it had remained mostly confined to the elite class and the religious establishment.

History

Bapudeva Sastri, holding globe, professor of astronomy, teaching a class at Queen's College, Varanasi, 1870

Sanskrit-based education comprising the learning of Vedic

to Gupta periods, coupled with the later Pali corpus of knowledge and a vast store of ancient to medieval learning in Persian/ Arabic languages, had formed the edifice of Hindu-Buddhist-Muslim education, till the rise of British power. But, the system became decadent as it missed the advancements that were taking place in Europe during and after the Renaissance, resulting in serious educational backwardness. Corrective measures were initiated by the British administration for making liberal, universal education available in this area through a network of schools to university system on the European pattern.

However, a real turning point came due to the efforts of educationalists like Pandit Madan Mohan Malviya and Sir Syed Ahmad Khan, who championed the cause of modern learning and supported British efforts to spread it.

Allahabad University, established 1887

Post-independence

Statue of Pandit Madan Mohan Malaviya at the entrance of Banaras Hindu University, established 1916

After independence, the state of U.P. has continued to make investment over the years in all sectors of education and has achieved significant success in overcoming general educational backwardness and illiteracy. The increase in overall literacy rate is due to persistent multi-pronged efforts made by the state government: to enrol and retain children, specially of weaker sections, in schools; to effectively implement the adult education programmes; and to establish centres of higher education. As a result, U.P. is ranked amongst the first few States to have successfully implemented the *Education For All* policy. The following is indicative of the gradual progress:

In 1981, the literacy rate in U.P. was 28% and it increased to 42% in 1991. In 1991, the adult literacy rate (per cent literates among those aged 15 and above) was 38% and increased to 49% in 1998, an increase of 11 per centage in the seven-year period. But, the differential between female and male literacy remained high: while in 1991, male literacy was 56% and female literacy 25%, eight years later in 1999, as per survey estimates, the male literacy became 73% and female literacy 43% (NFHS II).

One more notable feature in the state has been the persistence of higher levels of illiteracy in the younger age group, more so in females, especially in the rural areas. In the late 1980s, the incidence of illiteracy in the 10–14 age group was as high as 32% for rural males and 61% for rural females; and more than two-thirds of all rural girls in the 12–14 age group never went to school. Only 25% of the girls in 7+ age group were able to read and write in 1991 and this figure went down to 19% for rural areas: it was 11% for the scheduled castes, 8% for scheduled castes in rural areas and 8% for the entire rural population in the most educationally backward districts. In terms of completion of basic or essential educational attainment (the primary or the secondary education), in 1992–1993, only 50% of literate males and 40% of literate females could complete the cycle of eight years of schooling (the primary and middle stages). Possibly, Bihar is the only state in India which lags behind U.P. in education.

The problems of state's education system are complex. Due to public apathy the public schools are run inefficiently. Privately run schools (including those run by Christian missionaries) are functional, but expensive and so beyond the reach of ordinary people.

In order to make the population totally literate, steps are being taken by the government to involve public participation, including the help of NGOs and other organisations. There are also special programmes, like the World Bank aided DPEP. As a result, progress in adult education has been made and the census of 2001 indicates a male literacy rate of 70.23% and a female literacy rate of 42.98%.

Presently, there are 866,361 primary schools, 8,459 higher secondary schools, 758 degree colleges and 26 universities in the state. Some of the oldest educational institutions – founded by the British, the pioneer educationalists and other social/ religious reformers – are still functional.

In addition, a number of highly competitive ivy league centres of higher or technical education have been established since Independence.

HIGHER EDUCATION

Considering the size of Uttar Pradesh, it is not surprising that it has a large number of academic and research institutes. These institutes are either under the jurisdiction of the State Government, the Central Government, or are privately run. The state has two IITs – at Kanpur and Varanasi, an IIM at Lucknow, an LU at Lucknow, an NIT and an IIIT at Allahabad. A good number of State and Central Government universities are founded in Uttar Pradesh to provide Higher Education in various course works.

The Rajiv Gandhi Institute of Petroleum Technology: The Ministry of Petroleum and Natural Gas (MOP&NG), Government of India set up the institute at Jais, Rae Bareli district, Uttar Pradesh through an Act of Parliament. RGIPT has been accorded Institute of National Importance. With the status of a deemed university, the institute awards degrees in its own right. RGIPT is co-promoted as an energy domain specific institute by six oil public sector units (ONGC, IOCL, OIL, GAIL, BPCL and HPCL) in association with the Oil Industry Development Board (OIDB). The Institute is associated with leading International Universities/Institutions specializing in the domain of Petroleum Technology.

Alongside above mentioned institutes of higher learning, in Uttar Pradesh, a range of Government Degree College has been set up by the Government of Uttar Pradesh for providing Higher Education to scholars who are interested in different course work (undergraduate, postgraduate and research) and program (Humanities, Science and Commerce) in higher studies. At present in Uttar Pradesh, 137Government Degree Colleges has been established to fulfill the above criteria. The U.P. government administers and controls these colleges through Department of Higher Education, Uttar Pradesh; however, syllabus and affiliation to the universities concerned are depending upon the locality of Government Degree College. Beside government instructions, the government degree colleges also follow the norms and regulations of the University Grants Commission, New Delhi. Few private college likewise, IIMT Group of Institutions (Institute of Integrated Management and Technology) in Varanasi has been established. Uttar Pradesh Board of Technical Education is the body responsible for pre degree vocational and technical education.

Bab-e-syed, *the gateway to Aligarh Muslim University (AMU), established 1875*

EDUCATION AND SOCIAL WELFARE

Banaras Hindu University (BHU) is a Central University in Varanasi. It evolved from the Central Hindu College of Varanasi, envisioned as a Hindu university in April 1911 by Annie Wood Besant and Pandit Madan Mohan Malaviya. BHU began on 1 October 1917, with the Central Hindu College as its first constituent college.

Most of the money for the university came from Hindu princes, and its present 1,350-acre (5.5 km) campus was built on land donated by the Kashi Naresh. Regarded as one of the largest residential universities in Asia, it has more than 128 independent teaching departments; several of its colleges—including science, linguistics, law, engineering (IIT (BHU) Varanasi) and medicine (IMS-BHU)—are ranked amongst the best in India. The university's total enrolment stands at just over 15,000 (including international students). It is the only university in India hosting one of the IITs on its premises (IIT BHU).

The Indian Institute of Technology Kanpur (established in 1959 in the industrial city of Kanpur, and now known as IIT-Kanpur or IITK) is an Indian Institutes of Technology; it is primarily focused on undergraduate education in engineering and related science and technology, and research in these fields. It is among the few institutions which enjoys the status of an Institute of National Importance. IITK was the first college in India to offer education in computer science.

The Indian Institute of Technology (BHU) Varanasi traces its origins to three engineering and technological institutions established by Pandit Madan Mohan Malaviya in 1919–1923 in BHU. In 1971 these three colleges, viz. BENCO, MINMET and TECHNO, were merged to form the Institute of Technology (IT-BHU) and admissions were instituted jointly with the IIT's through the Joint Entrance Examination. In 2012, IT-BHU was officially rechristened as IIT (BHU) Varanasi. The institute has 13 departments and three inter disciplinary schools. It enjoys the status of an Institute of National Importance.

The Indian Institute of Management Lucknow was established in 1984 by the government of India. It was the fourth Indian Institute of Management to be established in India, after IIM Calcutta, IIM Ahmedabad and IIM Bangalore. IIM Lucknow's 185-acre (75 ha) main campus is in Prabandh Nagar, about 21 kilometres (13 mi) from Lucknow railway station and 31 kilometres (19 mi) from Lucknow Airport. A second campus, focusing on executive programs, was established in Noida. According to the institute's website, IIM Lucknow is the first IIM in the country to establish a second campus.

The Motilal Nehru National Institute of Technology, Allahabad (MNNIT) was formerly Motilal Nehru Regional Engineering College, Allahabad. It is among one of the leading institutes in the country, established in 1961 as a joint enterprise of the governments of India and Uttar Pradesh in accordance with the plan to establish regional engineering colleges. On 26 June 2002 the college became a deemed university and is now known as an Institute of National Importance. MNNIT was the first college in India to grant a Bachelor of Technology degree in computer science and engineering, and among the very few colleges in India to have a PARAM supercomputer.

The Rajiv Gandhi Institute of Petroleum Technology (RGIPT) in Jais, Raebareli was established by the Ministry of Petroleum and Natural Gas (MOP&NG) of the Government of India through an act of Parliament. RGIPT has been designated an Institute of National Importance, along with the Indian Institute of Technology (IIT) and Indian Institute of Management (IIM). With deemed university status, the institute awards degrees in its own right. RGIPT is co-sponsored as an energy-domain-specific institute by six oil public-sector units (ONGC, IOCL, OIL, GAIL, BPCL and HPCL), in association with the Oil Industry Development Board (OIDB). The institute is associated with international universities and institutions specialising in petroleum technology.

Rajiv Gandhi National Aviation University (RGNAU) is an autonomous public central university located in the Fursatganj Airfield, Rae Bareli, Uttar Pradesh.

Allahabad University is a Central University located in Allahabad. Its origins lie in Muir Central College, named after Lt. Governor of North-Western Provinces Sir William Muir in 1876; Muir suggested a Central University at Allahabad, which later evolved into the present institution. At one point it was called the "Oxford of the East", and on 24 June 2005 its Central University status was restored through the University Allahabad Act, 2005 of the Parliament of India. It is the fourth-oldest university in the country.

The Aligarh Muslim University is a residential academic institution. This university is spread over an area of 1.5 square kilometres (370 acres). Modelled on the University of Cambridge, it was established by Sir Syed Ahmed Khan in 1875 as Mohammedan Anglo-Oriental College and was granted the status of a Central University by an Act of Parliament in 1920. Located in the city of Aligarh, it was among the first institutions of higher learning established during the British Raj.

The Gautam Buddha University was established in 2002 by the Uttar Pradesh government. The university commenced its first academic session in 2008. It basically focusses on research and offers integrated dual-degree courses in engineering, biotechnology, Bsc, BBA+MBA, BBA+LLB, humanities and Buddhist studies. Its campus is spread over 511 acres and is located in Greater Noida in close proximity to many industrial units. The university has eight schools: Gautam Buddha University School of Engineering, Gautam Buddha University School of Information and Communication Technology, Gautam Buddha University School of Biotechnology, Gautam Buddha University School of Vocational Studies and Applied Sciences, Gautam Buddha University School of Management, Gautam Buddha University School of Law, Justice and Governance, Gautam Buddha University School of Buddhist Studies and Civilization and Gautam Buddha University School of Humanities and Social Sciences.

The Indian Institute of Information Technology, Allahabad was established in 1999 by the government of India. The institute was conferred deemed university status in 2000, empowering it to award degrees following the setting of its own examinations. The new campus has been developed on 100 acres (0.40 km) of land at Deoghat, Jhalwa, on the outskirts of Allahabad. The campus and other buildings have been styled on patterns developed by mathematics professor Roger Penrose. IIITA offers a BTech degree in both information technology and electronics and communications engineering. Admission is through the All India Engineering Entrance Examination (AIEEE). Foreign students are accepted based on SAT II scores. IIITA has an extension campus at Amethi, Sultanpur District (the Rajiv Gandhi Institute of Information Technology).

The Gautam Buddha Technical University is a well-known technical university, formerly known as Uttar Pradesh Technical University. It provides technical education, research and training in such programs as engineering, technology, architecture, town planning, pharmacy and applied arts and crafts which the central government decrees in consultation with All India Council for Technical Education (AICTE). There are five government engineering colleges of GBTU:

- Harcourt Butler Technological Institute, Kanpur
- Kamla Nehru Institute of Technology, Sultanpur
- Madan Mohan Malaviya Engineering College, Gorakhpur
- Institute of Engineering and Technology, Lucknow
- Bundelkhand Institute of Engineering & Technology, Jhansi

Other schools in the state capital, Lucknow, include Colvin Taluqdars' College, St. Francis' College, Lucknow and La Martinière College. Secondary schools include the Loreto Convent, St Agnes' Loreto High School and City Montessori School. The Babasaheb Bhimrao Ambedkar University, Lucknow is one of the youngest central universities in the country. The jurisdiction of this residential university is over the entire state of Uttar Pradesh. The campus Vidya Vihar is located off Rae Bareli Road, about 10 km south of the Charbagh railway station in Lucknow. All courses offered by the university are postgraduate, innovative and non-traditional.

M.J.P. Rohilkhand University, established in 1975, has produced a large number of scholars and technocrats in various fields of the arts, science and technology; it has departments of management, engineering, the arts, science, law, education and technology. The university's Institute of Engineering and Technology was established in 1995, and it has a successful job-placement bureau throughout India for graduating students.

- Harish-Chandra Research Institute, Allahabad : Harish-Chandra Research Institute (HRI) is a research institution, named after the mathematician Harish-Chandra, and located in Allahabad, Uttar Pradesh. It is an autonomous institute, funded by the Department of Atomic Energy (DAE), Government of India.

The Govind Ballabh Pant Social Science Institute, Allahabad: Established in 1980 as one in the network of Social Science Research Institutes, which Indian Council of Social Science Research (ICSSR) set up in association with the State Governments, in G.B.Pant's case,the Government of Uttar Pradesh.The Institute undertakes interdisciplinary research in the field of social sciences. G.B.Pant Institute entered privileges of the University of Allahabad in 2005. Govind Ballabh Pant Social Science Institute became a Constituent Institute of the University of Allahabad on 14 July 2005, when the University of Allahabad Act, 2005 came into force.

The main areas of research at the Institute include development planning and policy, environment, health and population, human development, rural development and management, culture, power and change, democracy and institutions.

Institute offers a doctoral programme in social sciences and a MBA in rural development MBA-RD programme. In both programmes the degree is awarded by the University of Allahabad.

Primary and secondary education

Most schools in the state are affiliated to Uttar Pradesh Madhyamik Shiksha Parishad (commonly referred to as U.P.

board) with English or Hindi as the medium of instruction, while schools affiliated to Central Board of Secondary Education (CBSE) and Council for the Indian School Certificate Examinations (CISCE) with English as medium of instruction are also present.

DISTANCE EDUCATION

A sustainable system of in-service teacher training linked to its Pedagogical Improvement Programme has been evolved using Distance Education technology. To achieve this, State Project Office (SPO) took up activities for development and production of distance learning material that can provide continuous support to teachers at their work place. The Govt. of India identified Indira Gandhi National Open University (IGNOU) to assist DPEP States in developing the Distance Education Programmme. A State Coordinator for Distance Education was appointed to facilitate work in this direction. The coordinator is located within and is in close association with the Pedagogy Unit of the SPO. This is proving useful for coordination and systematic interventions of the distance education component in the quality improvement programme under DPEP.

The State Institute of Education Technology (SIET), Lucknow remains closely involved in the Distance Education Programme of DPEP. The Institute houses expertise in handling scripts, editing and developing audio-video materials.

Focus : Supporting teachers through distance learning material and modes. (audio, video, print telecast, radio teleconferencing & video teleconferencing) giving :

- exposure to working modules or systems.
- example of actual material teachers can use with children to enhance their own understanding.
- response to their difficulties as they try to change.

Management

- Synchronised with DPEP's inservice teacher training programme & the Pedagogical Improvement Plan.

- Distance Education (DE) Coordinator in place-integrated with pedagogy unit.
- Core group of DE in existence. State Resource Group (SRG) also used. Close coordination with SIET.

Facilities

- Requisite audio-visual equipment + DDRS installed in all DPEP II and III DIETs.
- SIET houses all production facilities for audio-video multimedia programmes.

State Plan of Distance Education

The State Project Office organised a scheme to explore and identify possibilities of distance education to support and strengthen on-going teacher training programme. The exercise focused on needs of teacher training, primary school curriculum and the role of other academic support institutions like DIETs, BRCs, CRCs. Teleconferencing, video programmes, self instructional material, dovetailed with the on-going teacher training schedule were identified as modes for strengthening and enriching training programme through distance education. A State Work Plan was evolved having the following activities:

- Capacity Building of Institutions and individuals for the use of Distance Education technology.
- Orientation of core group.
- Supply of equipments facilitating use for D.E. material such as T.V., VCR, STD, FAX, Generator, Two-in-one, etc., to DIETs.
- Providing 'down link' or 'talk back' facility to each DIET for teleconferencing.

Training of Script Writers

- Production of software
- Field trials of software and modification
- Capacity Building for educational personnel :

- A group of 100 DIET Lecturers trained by Space Application Centre, Indian Space Resource Organization in use of hardware of Teleconferencing and conduct of these. They have been designated as learning end managers.
- Training imparted to 6 person from SPO, SIET, DIET, SIEMAT by Space Application Centre, ISRO, Ahmedabad to manage teaching end in Teleconferencing.
- 3 persons from SPO/SIET/ trained dy National Institute of Design, Ahmedabad in use of new media in education.
- 5 persons trained by Azim Premji Foundation Wipro to prepare CDROMs.

Integration of Existing Video Programme with Teacher Training: A user guide for existing video programmes available at SIET, Lucknow is developed. The video programmes have been duplicated and distributed to all DPEP-II districts for use in teachers training at BRC level.

BRIEF DEVELOPMENT

Content briefs for video programmes relevant to teacher training and revised primary school curriculum are developed by the State Resource Group (curriculum, text-book and training). These content briefs have been used by SIET for video programme production.

AUDIO-VIDEO MATERIALS

Koshish : A video film (Koshish - 11 minutes) documenting an innovative practice of organising teacher training sessions at BRC in the presence of children through actual demonstration by Assistant Coordinator, BRC in Eliya block of Sitapur district is made for BRC, NPRC coordinators.

'Sabal' Video Package : The programme tells how to organize and run teacher training programme.

PRINTED MATERIALS

Shikshakodaya : Self Instructional Material on various pedagogical issues such as how children learn, teacher, teaching learning methods etc. is developed in the workshop mode. The workshop also helped 22 participants to develop their skills in designing Self Instructional Material (SIM).

These SIMs have been printed and distributed to all teachers of Bareilly district and in the 2 blocks of Badaun district.

Newsletter enrichment—Abhivaykti : To enrich and make DIET Newsletters responsive to the needs of teachers, newsletter enrichment workshops were organized. Issues regarding subject, quality of content matter, layout, designing and production, were discussed in detail. The detailed document on newsletter preparation and production was developed & circulated to all DIET, BRC, NPRCs.

Identification of difficulty areas in Mathematics and development of SIM 'Sopan":

Concept of 'Zero', 'place value', 'borrowing and carryover', 'fraction' and 'language difficulties in maths' were identified as difficult areas by a group of primary school teachers & members of the SRG.

Self Instructional materials as support material for the teleconferencing on areas identified as difficult, is developed by the text book writers group on mathematics for primary classes with the help of SIM experts from Indira Gandhi National Open University, New Delhi.

Self instructional material developed for use of teachers has been printed by all DIETs and their distribution is completed through NPRC based monthly meetings.

Newsletter Publication: Quality of interaction and communication among teachers and trainers and between different levels of academic support units has changed significantly since the schools, BRCs, DIETs and State have begun to bring out their newsletters. These educational newsletters originating from different levels are providing a much wider forum to teachers and trainers to express their views and share views of others. These newspapers have also established a feed back mechanism for providing state a greater insight in local level educational strengths and weakness, success stories and failures.

While Shaikshik Prakshak is being brought out by SPO, 'Udaan', "Pratichhaya" are being brought out by DIETs Bareilly and Firozabad respectively. There are more such letters being published from other districts. BRC Dumariyaganj has made a poineer effort in bringing out a monthly newsletter 'Shiksha Darpan'. At village level schools are also having their wall newspapers for kids and neo-literate named Kankaiya, Gulgula, Patang etc..

Apart from general educational development, these newsletters are addressing a variety of issues catering to different needs of kids and teachers ranging from quiz, puzzle, success stories to guidelines for lesson planning and development of TLM. The aim is to focus problems that kid and teachers face every day while teaching and learning.

Leadership Training of Head Teachers : Looking at need that the head teacher plays a key role in growth of school and teaching learning process, it was decided that head teachers need to undergo training to upgrade their skills as head teacher, administrator and a link between school and community. A training module for leadership training of Head-teachers is prepared by SIEMAT and DEP, DPEP, IGNOU. Trialling of module has taken place at DIET Fatehpur in the Nov. last. Actual training of head teachers is planned at BRC level in cascade mode beginning from next year.

"Story Telling: Workshop September 11-13, 2002: A "story telling: workshop was organised from September 11 to 13, 2002 in which SRG members, story teller from community participated.

This workshop carried further the commitment towards the ordinary child who goes to a regular government school. An effort has also been made to involve the community in story-telling activity so as to ensure due space to the community heritage and recognize its important role in the education of children. All this is took place within the framework of improving the quality of education for primary school children throughout the state.

The workshop highlighted the purpose and effects of telling stories, so that children's interests and curiosity can be aroused, their imaginative faculties can develop, which would create an environment for further education, and improving their concentration as well as give space to their affective aspect. An effort was made to address questions such as: Why at all do we need stories? What kind of stories? How and where can stories be used, so as to facilitate classroom learning? Certain precautions pertaining to story selection, narration and inferences were also discussed.

The workshop aimed at evolving a group of storytellers and promoting pedagogical understanding of stories and their use across the state. Selection of good stories, and development of supplementary readers including audio cassettes of good stories are also under consideration. Guidelines have been identified on the art of story-telling and its use so that classroom learning can be maximised and a holistic approach to learning be implemented. The similar type of workshops will be organized across all the districts to elucidate to school teachers and community advantages of story telling and help them to identify good local and contextual children's literature set into the diversity of the state. Later these collection of stories will be made available to all children. These workshops are planned to start from December 2002.

USE OF RADIO TO PROVIDE ACADEMIC SUPPORT TO TEACHERS

Radio is the most popular means of reaching the unreached in rural areas. To use radio for giving academic support to teachers, following activities were taken:

- Educational broadcasts for primary school teachers already being produced by All India Radio (AIR) made relevant & responsive to the needs of class rooms in view of introduction of new text books in UP.
- A taskforce under the leadership of the Senior Professional (pedagogy) at SPO was constituted to focus on :

- Content and relevance of ongoing children's programmes specially with regards to introduction of new text books programmes for teachers on innovative and interesting teaching practices and methodology as per requirements of new text books
- A core group of 20 was set up. This includes people from SRG, AIR and SIET and has undergone training from the experts from EMPC, IGNOU, New Delhi and AIR in audio script writing.

ORIENTATION OF WRITERS FOR RADIO SCRIPT WRITING

A five day workshop was organised for DIET personnel to receive training in audio formats for designing radio scripts. These participants were drawn from those districts which house a DIET and a Radio Station.

Training in various formats of educational audio programmes such as talks, interviews, discussions, quiz, radio drama, documentary, reports, commentary were given to participants. Participants were given actual exposure to audio recording. Experts from AIR, New Delhi, EMPC IGNOU, New Delhi, AIR, Lucknow facilitated the workshop.

TRAINING OF FACILITATORS FOR TELECONFERENCING

All DIETs under DPEP-II & III participated and were oriented in ways and means to arrange a successful teleconferencing at DIETs by National level experts from Indian Space Resource Organization (ISRO) Ahmedabad.

Two hours of highly interactive teleconferencing was organised with 18 DIETs of BEP and DPEP districts on Sept 1, 2000. Activity based teaching learning, to prepare and use TLM in class and in multigrade situations, what changes are visible to supervisors after 2 rounds of teacher training, were discussed in detail. About 37 questions asked from 12 DIETs were handled in a 1 hr question-answer session.

Teleconferencing on Community Ownership of Schools: Three Teleconferencing to underlining importance of Community Participation have been organized on July 223 & Nov. 1,2002 Sept. 7, 2002 in which DIET faculty, teachers, BSA, BRC/NPRC participated.

A teleconferencing was organized on November 1, 2002 on theme of "Community Participation in UP." Through this VECs, Gram Pradhans, members of MTA, PTA, WMG, Primary school teachers and education officers got an opportunity to talk to Secretary, Govt. of India, Elementary Education and Literacy Sri S.C. Tripathi about their experiences and experiments, their achievement and handicaps in making the school a conducive place for children's learning.

As per interactive session data, 27 centres participated in the programme and about 1350 people attended the programme at the receiving end. The other panelists included Vice Chancellor IGNOU, Prof. Dixit, Joint Secretary, Govt. of India, Elementary Education Sri Sumit Bose, State Project Director, Mrs. Zohra Chatterji, Education For All Project Board, Director, DEP, DPEP, IGNOU, Sri SVS Chaudhary and Senior Professional, Community Participation Sri V K Pandey.

VIDEO-CONFERENCING

A Demo of Video-Conferencing with four districts Gorakhpur, Kanauj, Sonbhadra, Agra on "Literacy day" was organised on Aug 31, 2002, in which, Districts Magistrate DIET faculty, BSA, District coordinators participated.

FREE TEXT BOOKS DISTRIBUTION

In UPDPEP II, UPDPEP III, Janshala (Lucknow) and Sarva Shiksha Abhiyan Programme, there is a provision of free text book distribution to all girls and schedule caste and schedule tribe boys studying in parishadiya primary, upper primary and government schools.

Free Textbook Distribution System: The Directorate of Basic Education which houses the State Text book office is responsible for ensuring the timely printing and distribution of the Free text-books and timely availability of text books in the market.

- Specifications of the Job are finalised by the Government of Uttar Pradesh and communicated to the Director, Basic Education and the State Text Book Officer (State text book office).
- Technical and financial bids are invited for inner text and cover page separately through National Tendering process.
- A tender committee with the Director, Basic Education, as the Chairperson is constituted with State Textbook officer as the Member Secretary. After the publishers and printers are short listed by the committee on the basis of their technical bids, their financial bids are assessed and the final selection is made.
- The lowest price quoted by the successful bidder becomes the cost prize for all other successful bidders who agree to work on that lowest price. The price fixed includes the cost of paper, printing, transportation up to the district headquarters in case of textbooks for free distribution, binding, purchase of the textbook cover. Transportion cost is borne by the wholesaler and retailer for books that are sold in the market. The Printers/Publishers give 7.5% discount on the price of the book for free distribution and 1.5 royalty to Govt. through State Text-Book Office for the number of books for which agreement is made.
- In order to check the number of copies of textbooks to be printed and right amount of royalty to be paid, printing of the covers is entrusted to private Security presses accredited by the Reserve Bank of India.
- Each of selected printers is allocated a unique code. This code has to appear near the spine of every textbook printed by the Printers. This serves the dual purpose of monitoring the quality of the printing job by every printer and also reduces the possibility of unauthorised copies of the textbooks from reaching the market.

- Printers/publishers are given the manuscript on CD-Roms and the corresponding hard copies of the textbooks. In this way, the processing time at the printers end is eliminated and they are in a position to prepare the positives and negatives of the print material, plate making etc. to start printing work immediately. For books which are not given on CD Roms, the printers/publishers are required to make a model copy and get it approved by the subject specialists positioned in State Text book office and the Tender committee.
- After the printing job is over and the end product is verified for conformity with quality standards laid down for the job, every publishers/printer has to submit alteast five finished copies of the textbook printed by them to Assistant Director (Basic) of that Region and EBSA of that district.

An Evaluation Committee checks various aspects of quality along the guidelines provided by the Textbook Office. Under DPEP III programme the State Project Office, UP Education For All Project Board has strengthened the State Textbook Office and State textbook officer has purchased 10 paper testing (GSM) machine to check quality of paper at time of releasing of the textbooks.

Once text books clear quality test to meet the standards of quality control and the specified number of copies are found to match print order, the AD (Basic) and Basic Shiksha Adhikari releases the books for sale in the districts and for free distribution.

MICROPLANNING HOUSE HOLD SURVEY

Concepts: The needs and problems of a village are best known to its residents. The planners at the district/State/ national levels may not be well aware of the needs and problems of villages and also the priorities of the villagers. Hence, it is needed that villagers themselves should plan for their betterment and these plans be transmitted to authorities at district/state/ national levels. On the basis of these plans, work plans are these be prepared for block/district and state. This method has been named as decentralised planning. The data of every House Hold is collected for village level planning.

Need: No one except the villagers can really understand the needs and problems of a village and they themselves can give different methods/suggestions for fulfilment of the needs. These would give two benefits : one, they would be receptive to the plans the projects made by themselves because of emotional of attachment and second, would have active cooperation and participation in their implementation.

The villagers discuss smallest needs and problems of the village on basis of its relevance. During sruvey, many things are openly discussed such as education system of the village, quality of education enrolment of all children. The villagers become sensitive and also aware of educational issues and problems. After this, they participate in microplanning.

Method : An open meeting of members of village education committee along with energetic youths of the village, teachers, local non governmental organisations such as Nehru Yuvak Kendra, Yuvak Mangal Dal and others is convened where all small/big problems/needs are discussed and priorities draun.

Steps in House Hold Survey: Collection of information on village education register (Bal Garna Register) by the member of VEC.

- Making plan for cent percent enrolment of children for village school.
- Involvement of each girl/boy of the village with village education system.

Results of House Hold Survey

- Number of girls and boys going to the school.
- Number of girls and boys not going to the school.
- Number of children in different social groups.
- Number of girls and boys going to the board schools/ recognized schools/alternative schools/ECCE centres.

- Number of families whose children do not go to schools.
- Number of children with disabilities

Prioritization of Educational and other Problems/ Needs of the Village : Inhabitants of the village assemble at a place and prepare a list of all small and big problems and needs of the village. For this work, each person has also to write methods/solutions for atleast five problems/needs of the village.

Stages in House Hold Survey: There are four steps which are given below:

- *Family Survey:* At first a survey team consisting of teachers, members of village education committee and energetic persons of the village is established who collect complete information regarding each family of the village. For this, prescribed blankform is made available. All filled forms are collected after the survey. The main object of family survey is not only to collect information but also to highlight the need of education for villagers and also make villagers aware and responsible for village education system. Further, out of school children are identified in this survey.
- *Analysis of Information:* After survey of each family and school mapping, members of village education committee study the information thus collected and also the school mapping so that they are aware of the realities of their village education.

Collection of Information: Formats have been developed for consolidation and analysis of statistics made available by HHS through different levels : village panchyat, block, district and state. This information collected at block level on prescribed form at the district level which is then transmitted state headquarters.

INTEGRATED EDUCATION FOR DISABLED (IED)

The education and training of individuals with disabilities has undergone many changes. A person, who is severely impaired, never knows her/his own hidden sources of strength until she is not treated like a human being and encouraged to shape her/his own life. Integrated Education for Disabled (IED) is the education of disabled children in the regular classrooms. It refers to the opportunity for children with special needs to participate fully in all the educational activities that typify every society.

Objectives

- To provide least restrictive environment to disabled children so that they may grow and develop like other children.
- To integrate the children with mild to severe disabilities to formal Govt. schools.
- Parent/Sibling Conselling
- To support manpower development activities and train required personal such as normal school teachers, DIET lecturers and itinerant teachers.
- To setup resource centres.
- To provide an equal opportunity to the disabled children and prepare them for life like other members of the society.
- To mainstream the disabled children to achieve principle of normalization.

U.P. EDUCATION FOR ALL PROJECT BOARD

The Government of India under National Education Policy of 1986 (as updated in 1992) and the Programme of Action 1992 reaffirm national commitment to universalisation of elementary education (means education upto class eighth). Para 5.12 of NPE resolves that free and compulsory education of satisfactory quality should be provided to all children upto 14 years of age before we enter the 21st century.

Keeping above in view, a World Bank assisted project called Basic Education Project had been undertaken in 1993, for expansion of quality basic education in the state. For smooth running of this project, a society "Uttar Pradesh Sabhee Ke Liye Shiksha Pariyojana Parishad (U.P. Education for all Project Board) has been established on 17 May, 1993 under Societies Registration Act of 1860. It's objectives are :-

The Parishad shall act as an autonomous and independent body for implementation of the Uttar Pradesh Education For All Project (Hereinafter referred to as "the Project") as outlined in the Project Document published by the Government of Uttar Pradesh and its revised version that may be prepared on the basis of review from time to time. The activities of the Parishad will be concentrated in selected districts, but may extend to the whole State of U.P. in respect of selected and sponsored projects.

The Parishad has been established to function as a societal mission for bringing about a fundamental change in the basic education system, and through it in the overall socio-cultural situation. The following specific objectives of the Project would be pursued by the Parishad:

- Universalisation of Primary Education, viewed as a composite programme of (i) access to primary education for all children up to 14 years of age; (ii) universal participation till they complete the primary stage through formal or non-formal education programmes; and (iii) universal achievement atleast of the minimum levels of learning.

Provision of continuing education and skill development programmes for youth.

Making suggestions for greater gender equality in education and female empowerment.

Making necessary intervention to provide equal educational opportunity to children belonging to the Scheduled Castes, Scheduled Tribes and the poorest sections of society.

Laying special emphasis on all educational activities on culture and communication; science and environment and inculcation of a sense of social justice.

The district primary education programme-II was started in 1997 in 22 districts of the state which ended in 2003. Moreover, DPEP-III was started in 32 districts of the state in 2000 and has ended on 31 March, 2006.

Janshala project was implemented in district Lucknow during 2000-2003.

Sarva Shiksha Abhiyan was started in the state in 16 districts in 2001-2002 and now covers all 70 districts of the state.

GIRLS EDUCATION

Girls who comprise almost one half of the eligible child population, fall into category of children requiring special attention as their participation in primary education has been unsatisfactory. In this context, it must be realized that the participation level trends are not up to mark in the case of special social groups such as scheduled castes, tribes and minorities, other backward castes etc. The Primary schools have clearly indicated that girls enrolment and retention have been low as compared to boys and this has widened gender gap. Therefore, to combat such situations, different interventions are being adopted for expansion of education for girls

Strategies

(A) Maa-Beti Mela and Women Parliament

Objectives : Creating awareness about importance of girls education, for this purpose relevant material is being widely disseminated.

Orienting mothers about importance and significance of education for girls.

Putting in place a functional relationship between the teachers and parents.

Drawing attention of teachers towards problems of girls.

Holding discussions on gender concerns and trying to change peoples' attitudes towards their daughters and sons. Efforts are, thus, made to sensitize them and make them realize how their negative disposition prevents daughters form coming out of their shells.

Holding discussions on present education system and appealing to those present to participate in making it more effective and responsive to expressed needs.

(B) *Model Cluster Development Approach (MCDA):* Specific strategies for girls are being adopted in certain areas of the project districts. One such strategy is the MCDA, which focuses on to improved participation of girls in Primary Education.

Crieteria for Selection of the Clusters

Low female literacy rate.

Poor enrolment and retention of girls.

Dominance of minority or Scheduled Castes / Other Backward Castes population

Clusters having 10-12 villages.

Presence of active Village Education Committees.

Presence of some active women's groups or motivated individuals:

(C) *Gender Sensitization Of Teachers:* All districts and block level educational functionaries being provided inputs of gender sensitization.

Orientation and training programmes are being conducted to sensitize teachers, BRCC-NPRCC for gender sensitive classroom processes as well as to make supervisory functionaries more gender sensitive.

To increase women participation in school management, mother teacher association (MTA) and parent teacher association (PTA) are being formed in schools.

Women motivator groups (WMG) are being formed in those villages where there is no school, or where inaccessibility to the school exists especially for girls or where there are scattered hamlets and where number of out of school children especially girls is alarming.

(D) *Retention Strategies:* A specific retention strategy is developed which has envisaged combined effort of the community, the teachers and the grass-root level functionaries to achieve goal. Monthly marking are given to the children using coloured stars. Retention marches are another effort among the retention improvement initiatives.

(E) *Summer Camps:* Important initiative is to bring back drop-out girls to the school. It was decided to organize summer camps for these girls which would make them fit to be enrolled subsequently in formal schools as per their achievement levels.

(F) *Meena Campaign:* A special intervention to develop community commitment for girl's education has been initiated under DPEP. It uses audio-visual material on Meena developed by UNICEF. Menna Campaigns are being organized with the objective of sensitizing community on issues related to girls education, so that supportive environment for girls education is created at the community level

(G) *Meena Manch:* Was organized at State Institute of Education Management and Training (SIEMAT), Allahabad on 12-14 August, 2002 in which approximately 60 participants from various fields participated. A second follow-up workshop was inaugurated at SIEMAT by the Basic Education Minister of the state on 15th November, 2002.

"Meena" symbol of the girl child and the spokesperson for girls education and girls rights developed by UNICEF, is being launched in a big way in the state, video cassettes of the Meena films have been provided to all the district headquarters and are being regularly shown. A workshop\to spread Meena Campaign to the grassroots level, the concept of organizing girls into clubs called "Meena Manch" has been recently developed. The objectives of these clubs are as follows:

to provide a platform for self-expression by the girl child.

to develop a spirit of leadership & cooperation.

resolution of adolescent doubts & queries.

to mainstream all girls into schools.

to inculcate, reading habits & develop creativity.

Skill development & life skills.

awareness generation regarding nutrition, health, sanitation and organization of related activities at village level.

awareness regarding women's rights & opposition of child marriage.

to encourage the savings habit.

10 such clubs are being formed in each district for which support from the project is being provided as below:

1. Membership fees of 20 'founder members' Rs. 20
2. Opening of bank account Rs. 80
3. Set of 'Meena' story-books Rs. 120
4. National Book Trust membership and books Rs. 100
5. Meena badge (to be provided by UNICEF)
6. Cupboard
7. Handwoven Carpet (Dari) - to be provided by community

All the district coordinators (girls education) have been briefed at headquarters about how to organize the clubs. A time bound schedule has been prescribed culminating in the organization of "Ma-Beti melas" across the state on 30th November, 2002 during which the following office bearers of the executive committee of "manch" will be selected.

- Chairman
- Secretary
- Treasurer
- Two members

The executive committee will meet once a month and work actively to increase membership and organize monthly activities. A girl with ability to speak well & motivate others will be selected as "Meena Prerak" or "Meena motivator". She will be the chief spokesperson of the club.

The themes for monthly activities have been prescribed for the whole year and a guide book is being developed for the same. The first month will be devoted to self-expression. In the second month, a skill development and income generating activity will be selected by the girls with the assistance of resource persons. This will be taught to the girls and continue as a standard activity throughout the year till the girls wish to learn a new skill. In addition to this, events and activities will be planned around the theme for the month.

It is hoped that this Manch will develop as an effective platform for inculcating a strong leadership & missionary zeal amongst the girls for creating a better-educated life & environment for themselves & society in the future.

SHIKSHA MITRA

Shiksha Mitra Scheme as para teachers for U.P. Basic Shiksha Parishadiya Primary Schools.

Need

- Universalization of elementary education.
- Non availability of minimum 2 teachers for each parishadiya primary schools.
- Deployment problem in rural interior schools.
- Teacher Pupil Ratio is very high in rural areas. To maintain teacher pupil ratio as per norms in remote areas.
- To involve VEC support in primary education.

Objectives of the Scheme

- To provide minimum two teachers in each parishadiya primary school.
- To minimise the teacher pupil ratio up to the norms.
- To make provision for local youths to serve their community.
- To ensure active participation of Village Education Committee in primary education.
- To make provision for local educated ladies to serve in schools & promote Community confidence in girls education.
- To increase retention of children.

- To ensure enrolment of out of school children by focussing Shiksha Mitras on largest classes I & II in schools.
- To obtain, aim of five teachers per school, in 3:2 ratio of regular teachers & Shiksha Mitras.

Assumption of Shiksha Mitra Scheme: It is a Government of Uttar Pradesh scheme & applicable to all Parishadiya Primary Schools since 1 July, 2000.

1. Willing & qualified teachers are not available for primary schools in remote village of backward areas.
2. Arrangement for primary education through young persons having education up to Intermediate belonging to the same village and willing to serve the community.
3. Local person through rigorous training can serve and teach up to class 2nd easily.

Operational Aspects of the Shiksha Mitra Scheme : Minimum educational qualification for the Shiksha Mitra as Intermediate or equivalent.

- Shiksha Mitras should be from the village, failing which from the Nayaya Panchayat where the primary school is located.
- 50% women will be selected as Shiksha Mitra.
- Selection will be done by Village Education Committee (VEC) through merit list prepared on the basis of average of educational qualification marks obtained at High School & Intermediate level, B.Ed's given priority.
- Selected list of Shiksha Mitra will be screened by the District Level Committee, to check that it is as per rules and then only honorarium funds will be released to VEC & Shiksha Mitra sent for one month pre-inducation training.
- After approval of the District Level Committee, the selected candidates have to obtain an month rigorous training at DIETs.
- Rs. 2250/- is the honorarium p.m. paid through VEC.

- Shiksha Mitra can be removed from his duty by VEC due to non-satisfactory performance.
- Shiksha Mitra entrusted to teach class - I & II. They are trained specifically for this.
- Rigorous training for 30 days is provided on the basis of training module prepared by the experts & educationists of State Council of Educational Research and Training.
- A provision of 15 days refresher training after completion of every year academic session successfully, and the V.E.C.'s renewal of his candidature for next session.
- Teaching Learning Material grants have been provided to Shiksha Mitras also for joyful learning practices.
- VEC can reappoint the Shiksha Mitra in next session keeping in view their work & conduct.

Sanctioned Shiksha Mitra

- Total 18147 Shiksha Mitras were sanctioned in DPEP districts in year 2000-01 out of which 17300 have been selected and are placed in schools.
- 18994 Shiksha Mitras sanctioned by Directorate of Basic Education in year 2001-02, for which selection process is going on.
- 19690 Shiksha Mitras have been sanctioned in mid 2001-02 for DPEP-II, III & Sarva Shiksha Abhiyan for which the selection process is going on.
- 2052 Shiksha Mitras are going to be sanctioned in this year 2002-03 for DPEP-II & III.

General Impact of the Scheme

- Single teacher schools have been reduced from 17% to 4%.
- Public perception of Shiksha Mitra's work is very good.
- Head Teachers & regular teachers are reporting that teaching work done by Shiksha Mitra of good quality.

- There are more lady teachers in schools - 40% are Shiksha Mitras.
- Highly qualified Shiksha Mitra's having qualification up to postgraduate & B.Ed. are getting selected.
- Children of class I & II are responding well to the local Shiksha Mitra in the play way method.
- Shiksha Mitra's are benefitting from monthly Nyay Panchayat Resource Centre (NPRC) meetings with regular teachers.

Bibliography

Ali, Tariq: *An Indian Dynasty: The Story of the Nehru-Gandhi Family*, New York, Putnam, 1985.

Anthony, J. Parel : *Hind Swaraj or Indian Home Rule*, Cambridge University Press, 1925.

Bahadur, Prasad, Lal : *Indian Political System and Law*, New Delhi, Shree, 2005.

Baird, Robert: *Religion in Modern India*, New Delhi, Manohar, 1981.

Basham, A.L.: *A Cultural History of India*, Oxford, Clarendon Press, 1975.

Desai, Mahadev : *Gandhi and Indian Villages*, New Delhi, Mohit Pub., 2002.

Farquhar, J.N.: *Modern Religious Movements in India*, Munshiram, New Delhi, 1967.

Frauwallner, E..: *History of Indian Philosophy*, Motilal, Delhi, 1973.

Grisenold, H.D.: *Insights into Modern Hinduism*, Oxford, New York, 1934.

James, Lawrence: *The Rise and Fall of the British Empire*, St. Martin's, 1997.

Jane A. Bullock : *Introduction to Emergency Management*, Amsterdam, Butterworth-Heinemann, 2003.

Kalika Prasad Tiwari: *Foundations of Ancient Indian Culture*, Pointer Publishers, Delhi, 2001.

Karmarkar, D.: *Sankara's Advaita*, Karnatak University, Dharwar, 1976.

Kumari, R. : *Women-Headed Households in Rural India*, New Delhi, Radiant Publishing, 1989.

Levinson, D.: *Family Violence in Cross Cultural Perspective*, Newbury Park, Sage, 1989.

Mayer, A.: *Caste in an Indian Village: Change and Continuity 1954-1992*, Delhi, OUP, 1996.

Metcalf, Thomas R.: *Modern India: An Interpretive Anthology*, London, Macmillan, 1971.

Minakshi, C.: *Administration and Social Life under the Pallavas*, Madras, University of Madras, 1977.

Misra, Satya Swarup: *The Aryan Problem: A Linguistic Approach*, Munshiram Manoharlal, New Delhi, 1992.

Parel , J.: *Hind Swaraj or Indian Home Rule*, Cambridge University Press, 1925.

Ram, Jagivan: *Caste Challenge in India*, New Delhi, Vision Books, 1980.

Richard Davis: *Lives of Indian Images,* Princeton Univ. Press. Princeton, 1997.

Roubos- Bennett, M. : *Redefining Disasters: A Decade of Counter Disaster Planning,* State Library of New South Wales, Sydney, 1996.

Schwartz, Cowan, Ruth: *A Social History of American Technology.* New York: Oxford University Press, 1996.

Seyla Benhabib: *The Reluctant Modernism of Hannah Arendt*, Rowan and Littlefield Publishers, 2003.

Shashipriya Dei: *Development of Temple Architecture in India*, Punthi-Pustak, Delhi, 1998.

Singh, Harbans: *The Heritage of the Sikhs*, Columbia, Missouri, South Asia Books, 1983.

Singh, M.N.: *Fundamentals of Indian Culture: A Modernistic View of Ancient Traditions*, Pratibha Prakashan, Delhi, 2010.

Sivaramamurti, C.: *Sri Lakshmi in Indian Art and Thought*, Kanak, New Delhi, 1982.

Sri Aurobindo: *The Foundations of Indian Culture*, Pondicherry, 1980.

Subhan, John A.: *Sufism: Its Saints and Shrines*, Lucknow, 1938.

Susan Huntington: *The Art of Ancient India,* Weatherhill, 1985.

Thakur, Ramesh Chandra, *Government and Politics of India*, New York, St. Martin's Press, 1995.

Thapar, Romila: *Cultural Pasts: Essays in Early Indian History,* New Delhi, India: Oxford University Press, 2000

Tobias, Michael: *A Day in the Life of India,* San Francisco, Collins Publishers San Francisco, 1996.

Index

www.ingramcontent.com/pod-product-compliance
Ingram Content Group UK Ltd.
Pitfield, Milton Keynes, MK11 3LW, UK
UKHW042016290726
14061UKWH00001BB/26